Enacting Differentiation in the Teacher Education Classroom

Enacting Differentiation in the Teacher Education Classroom

Practical Strategies for Modeling and Reflection

Sarah E. Pennington, PhD

BLOOMSBURY ACADEMIC
NEW YORK · LONDON · OXFORD · NEW DELHI · SYDNEY

BLOOMSBURY ACADEMIC
Bloomsbury Publishing Inc, 1359 Broadway, New York, NY 10018, USA
Bloomsbury Publishing Plc, 50 Bedford Square, London, WC1B 3DP, UK
Bloomsbury Publishing Ireland, 29 Earlsfort Terrace, Dublin 2, D02 AY28, Ireland

BLOOMSBURY, BLOOMSBURY ACADEMIC and the Diana logo are trademarks of
Bloomsbury Publishing Plc

First published in the United States of America 2026

Copyright © Sarah Pennington, 2026

Cover design by Kathi Ha
Cover image © iStock.com/malerapaso

All rights reserved. No part of this publication may be: i) reproduced or transmitted in any form, electronic or mechanical, including photocopying, recording or by means of any information storage or retrieval system without prior permission in writing from the publishers; or ii) used or reproduced in any way for the training, development or operation of artificial intelligence (AI) technologies, including generative AI technologies. The rights holders expressly reserve this publication from the text and data mining exception as per Article 4(3) of the Digital Single Market Directive (EU) 2019/790.

Bloomsbury Publishing Inc does not have any control over, or responsibility for, any third-party websites referred to or in this book. All internet addresses given in this book were correct at the time of going to press. The author and publisher regret any inconvenience caused if addresses have changed or sites have ceased to exist, but can accept no responsibility for any such changes.

Library of Congress Cataloging-in-Publication Data is available

ISBN: HB: 978-1-5381-9455-3
       PB: 978-1-5381-9456-0
       ePDF: 979-8-8818-5628-1
       eBook: 978-1-5381-9457-7

Typeset by Integra Software Services Pvt. Ltd.
Printed and bound in the United States of America

For product safety related questions contact productsafety@bloomsbury.com.

To find out more about our authors and books visit www.bloomsbury.com
and sign up for our newsletters.

Contents

List of Figures vii
List of Tables viii
Acknowledgments ix

Introduction 1
    What Is Differentiation (and What It Is Not) 1
    What DI Is Not 3
    Why Differentiation in the Teacher Education Classroom? 5
    Overcoming the Challenges to Move to Enactment and Reflection: About This Book 9

1 Introducing the Differentiated Classroom to Your Preservice Teachers 11
    What Is the Difference between Equal and Equitable? 12
    Not Everyone Has the Same Strengths (Artistic, Athletic, and Academic Subjects) 13
    Supporting PST Understanding of Differentiation 16
    Opportunities for Reflecting on DI in Teacher Education 19
    Reflection and Discussion Questions 26

2 How Assessment Supports Differentiated Instruction 29
    Pre-Assessments 31
    Instruction-Embedded Assessments 41
    Utilizing Assessment Results to Plan for Instruction 46
    Goal-Setting Strategies 50
    Reflection and Discussion Questions 54
    Additional Technology Tools for Assessment 56

3 Differentiation by Environment 59
Creating a Welcoming Classroom Environment 59
Strategies for Differentiation by Environment 65
Strategies to Set the Stage 71
Grouping Strategies to Encourage Student Interaction 75
Reflection and Discussion Questions 81

4 Differentiation by Content 85
Strategies for Differentiating by Content: Materials 86
Strategies for Differentiating by Content: Methods 88
Strategies for Content Differentiation and More 91
Reflection and Discussion Questions 98

5 Differentiation by Process 103
Strategies for Differentiation by Process 104
Reflection and Discussion Questions 120

6 Differentiation by Product 123
General Strategies 126
Specific Strategies and Tools 129
Reflection and Discussion Questions 152

7 Differentiated Instruction Across the Teacher Education Program: Building Faculty Capacity 155
Faculty Development 155
Program Design 159
Reflection and Discussion Questions 164

Appendix A: Graphic Organizer for Utilization of the Dual Role Reflection Model 168
Appendix B: Synthesis Reflection Questions for Instructors and Preservice Teachers 170
Appendix C: Preservice Teacher Questions for Reflecting on Differentiated Instruction within Clinical Placements 173
References 175
Index 188
Author Biography 193

Figures

1 Dual Role Reflection Model 21
2 Example Mind Map 40

Tables

1 Example Reflection Graphic Organizer 24
2 Example Vocabulary Chart 32
3 Example Anticipation Guide (Factual Knowledge) 33
4 Example Anticipation Guide B (Factual Knowledge) 34
5 Example Anticipation Guide (Attitude) 35
6 Example Completed K-W-L Chart 44
7 Example Triage Self-Assessment 45
8 Vocabulary Pre-Assessment Results 47
9 Example Task Chart 92
10 Example Learning Contract 96
11 Example Major Assignment Steps Checklist 106
12 Matrix Chart Example 118
13 Inquiry Chart Example 119
14 Possible Product Modalities for Differentiated Products 124
15 Example Rubric for RAFT Response 131
16 Example 100-Point Project Excerpt 134
17 Example Rubric: 100-Point Project Analytic Rubric 139
18 Tic-Tac-Toe Example 142
19 Single-Point Rubric for Tic-Tac-Toe Activity 146
20 Menu Example 148
21 Rubric for Menu Choice Board 150

Acknowledgments

Writing this book would not have been possible without the support, insight, and generosity of many people.

First, my deepest gratitude to J.D. for your unwavering encouragement and patience throughout this process. Your belief in me has made all the difference.

A heartfelt thank you to Ann Fox, Christina Fassbender, and Elizabeth Green for reading drafts of this book, offering thoughtful feedback, and helping me shape my ideas. Your insights and support strengthened this work in ways I could not have done alone.

To my colleagues, mentors, and students—your passion for education continues to inspire me, and I am grateful for the conversations and experiences that shaped the thinking behind this book.

And finally, to all the teachers who dedicate themselves to the learning and growth of their students—this book is for you.

Introduction

What Is Differentiation (and What It Is Not)

After each class meeting with the preservice teachers (PSTs) in my courses, I set aside a few minutes to read over their feedback and consider any adjustments I may need to make for future instruction. It is a reflective routine that I enjoy because it pushes me to move past my own perceptions regarding how class went and consider the thoughts of those who experienced it. One particular comment in my second year at my current institution made me stop in my tracks. I could almost hear the screech of brakes as I read it and thought, "Now, wait a minute! I know I…" before I stopped myself, shifted into reflective mode, and reread the comment.

"I totally get what the types of differentiation are. I have heard about content, process, and product differentiation in multiple classes. But I still don't know what it looks like or how to make it happen in practice."

I considered all the ways I had embedded opportunities for differentiation within my course thus far, ranging from varying modalities of content texts to the inclusion of multiple product choices from which students could select to show their developing knowledge and skills as an educator. I went through my course materials to see what was missing. I considered what I knew about pedagogy and supporting student learning. And I realized what was missing—I had expected students to independently *recognize* the strategies I was implementing as models of differentiation. I had not been explicit in naming and claiming the elements of differentiated instruction (DI) within my class, nor had I taken advantage of the opportunities to have the PSTs in my courses reflect on their own learning and engagement and how they were impacted by the strategies I was utilizing.

I followed up on this epiphany by speaking to colleagues about their own implementation of DI in courses within their teacher education programs (TEPs). Their responses echoed the comment of the PST in my course: they discuss it and offer basics on how to do it in their content area but do not always implement it and do not explicitly highlight it when they do so, a sentiment that is evidenced in research with PSTs who indicate they have learned about the theory related to DI but have not seen it utilized often (Sakellariou & Polyxeni, 2019). As one colleague shared, there were no immediate practical resources to support DI or reflection on its enactment in a higher-education setting. This book is a step toward remedying that gap so that PSTs can have opportunities to experience and reflect on DI and feel more confident implementing it in their own classrooms.

What Is DI? Clarifying Misconceptions

DI is defined as planning and adjusting instruction to meet the needs of diverse learners within the classroom (Tomlinson, 2017). It is not a single strategy but an instructional approach (some say a philosophy) that can utilize a variety of strategies (Watts-Taffe et al., 2012). The use of DI in the classroom provides students with multiple options for engaging with information and for expressing their understanding and learning (Tomlinson, 2017). In considering the use of DI in the classroom, teachers can differentiate in four broad areas: content (what the learners are engaging with or how material is presented), process (how the learners are engaging with content), product (what the learners create utilizing their new knowledge or skills or how they show what they have learned), and environment (the location in which the learners are engaging in learning as well as the creation of an emotionally safe learning environment; Tomlinson, 2017). However, a differentiated classroom does not require that all these elements of differentiation be present in every lesson, nor does it require that all differentiation be preplanned. Effective classroom differentiation can include both preplanned and "on the fly" differentiation (Parsons, Dodman, & Burrowbridge, 2013).

DI is an approach to teaching that requires teachers to consider student factors, including their readiness (current level of skills or knowledge), interests, strengths, challenges, and factors such as culture and context (D'Intino & Wang, 2021; Tomlinson, 2014). Thus, DI is a learner-centered approach that purposefully considers the supports students need to succeed (D'Intino & Wang, 2021) and requires teachers to know their students (van Geel et al., 2019). In addition, teachers must have strong pedagogical content knowledge to effectively differentiate, as effective planning and implementation of DI requires setting of content goals, the ability to connect to students' prior knowledge, and purposeful decision-making regarding the use of content-specific materials (Marks et al., 2021; van Geel et al., 2019). DI considers that each classroom will include learners with a variety of strengths, needs, backgrounds, and interests. Finally, as with all educational strategies or approaches, DI is not a magic bullet—it must be implemented thoughtfully and using data. Due to the extensive number of strategies that fall under the umbrella of DI as well as the number of misconceptions surrounding DI as an educational practice, research on DI as a teaching approach can be inconsistent. However, meta-analyses have found DI to have a small positive effect on student achievement in the elementary grades and a small to medium positive effect on student outcomes in secondary grades (van Geel et al., 2023). More research that focuses on specific strategies for DI and avoids misconceptions and neuromyths is needed.

What DI Is Not

DI is sometimes equated to individualized or personalized instruction. However, while these approaches may share some similarities, including the modification of curricula based on students' strengths and needs and the use of formative assessment to adjust instruction, there are some important differences (Kettler & Taliaferro, 2022). Key among these is the focus on planning instruction based on shared characteristics (e.g., background knowledge, readiness levels, and interests) among groups of students in DI as opposed to focusing on planning instruction for individual students within personalized or individualized learning (Kettler & Taliaferro, 2022).

This focus on meeting the needs of students through analysis of trends to differentiate can be less overwhelming than planning for each individual student while still meeting the needs of students who require varying levels of challenge and scaffolding. By differentiating content, process, and product for groups of students rather than designing entirely unique learning experiences for each individual, DI strikes a balance between responsiveness and feasibility. This can be particularly beneficial in classrooms with diverse learning needs, where it may not be practical for educators to create entirely separate lesson plans for each student. Instead, DI enables teachers to scaffold instruction, provide multiple pathways to learning, and create flexible groupings that evolve based on ongoing assessments, all of which contribute to a more inclusive and effective learning environment.

DI is also not providing instruction based on students' "learning styles." Although many educators still believe that individual students are kinesthetic or auditory learners (e.g., Nancekivell et al., 2020), "at present, there is no adequate evidence base to justify incorporating learning-styles assessments into general education practice" (Pashler et al., 2008, p. 105). Although it may seem like common sense that a student will perform better if material is presented in their preferred style, this approach is not supported by evidence (Cuevas, 2015; Pashler et al., 2008) and can be potentially harmful, as it promotes a fixed mindset in which students feel they cannot learn if material is not presented in a certain way (American Psychological Association, 2019). In truth, the best modality for learning content often depends on the content to be learned (Reiner & Willingham, 2010). In addition, providing opportunities for students to engage in content and processes that involve multiple modalities is important for supporting student learning, particularly as students engage in building twenty-first-century skills, such as complex problem-solving, communication, collaboration, and critical thinking (Geisinger, 2016).

Finally, DI is not "streaming" students into specific classes based on achievement in order to create consistent homogeneous groupings (Graham et al., 2021). At its heart, differentiation is a strategy for meeting the needs of students in a heterogeneous setting and should utilize flexible, dynamic grouping based on ongoing assessment to identify student needs. Thus, student groupings should be adjusted frequently utilizing ongoing assessment that recognizes student growth and provides opportunities for scaffolds and enrichment as needed.

Differentiation and Culturally Responsive Teaching

Culturally responsive teaching (CRT) engages teachers in instructional design that considers the diverse experiences, backgrounds, cultures, and strengths of the students in their classroom (Kieran & Anderson, 2019). Through this purposeful and proactive design, traditional barriers for students, such as modes of instruction, task types, and instructional materials utilized, can be removed or reduced (Kieran & Anderson, 2019). Among various practices within CRT are high expectations for all students, collaborative learning in the classroom, and multiple modes for students to share their knowledge (Kieran & Anderson, 2019). Classrooms informed by CRT also engage students' funds of knowledge (Moll et al., 1992) to provide opportunities for students to relate their own lives, experiences, and cultural ways of knowing to the skills and knowledge built within the classroom. This allows students to see themselves not just as consumers of knowledge but also as producers. CRT also requires the teacher to shift their role to allow for more student voice to engage students in purposeful ownership of their own learning while serving in more of a support role within a classroom that provides appropriate challenge for the students (Kieran & Anderson, 2019). These practices can be integrated with DI, adding in a level of purposeful knowledge and consideration of students' cultural backgrounds and the strengths and knowledge that accompany these. For example, in one New Zealand high school, Māori students were asked to use their knowledge of traditional Māori warrior burial practices to make predictions about burial practices for ancient Roman warriors (Hogg, 2016).

Why Differentiation in the Teacher Education Classroom?

Many teachers indicate that they feel underprepared for implementing DI in their classrooms (van Geel et al., 2019). Teachers express reasons for not implementing DI within their classrooms, including the time required (van Geel et al., 2022; Shareefa et al., 2019; Wan, 2017), lack of knowledge or experience (Altun & Nayman, 2022; van Geel et al., 2022; Shareefa et al., 2019; Wan, 2017), lack of materials (Altun & Nayman, 2022; Bondie et al., 2019; Shareefa et al., 2019), and pressures focused around standardized testing (Altun & Nayman, 2022; Bondie et al., 2019; Dack & Triplett, 2020). Teachers' likelihood of implementing DI within their classroom is positively associated with their DI self-efficacy (Suprayogi et al., 2017). In addition, research indicates that there is a positive relationship between teachers' comfort level with implementing DI and whether they have received specific training in DI (Bogen et al., 2019; Dixson et al., 2014). Thus, professional development is important for supporting teachers in the implementation of DI within their classrooms (Langelaan et al., 2024; Valiandes & Neophytou, 2018). However, research has found that some teachers view the professional development they have received around DI to be minimal (Porta & Todd, 2022).

PSTs echo the perceptions of practicing teachers, indicating that they feel unprepared to enact DI in the classroom (Scarparolo & Subban, 2021). Current research indicates multiple possible reasons for this perception of being underprepared, including lack of intentional and explicit modeling of DI in the TEP (Gibbs & Beamish, 2021; Ruys et al., 2013; Sakellariou & Polyxeni, 2019). Modeling DI in the TEP classroom can help clarify common misunderstandings about differentiation and help PSTs see differentiation as an achievable practice within the classroom (Dack, 2018; 2019; Roiha, 2023). This is further supported by research showing that PSTs who engaged in learning and application of the principles of DI indicated that they felt capable of preparing and utilizing differentiated activities in their future classrooms (Yenmez & Özpınar, 2017). Additional research also indicates that many PSTs view utilization of DI as one of the most important things that they need to learn in their TEP, second only to classroom management (Clark & Byrnes, 2015). To be most effective, the explicit modeling of DI within teacher education should be woven throughout the program as opposed to being part of a single course.

Considering the potential of DI strategies for supporting student achievement in areas such as reading (Puzio et al., 2020), science (Al-Sherhi, 2020), and mathematics (Goddard et al., 2019; Lai et al., 2020), it is important that teachers can effectively implement DI. To meet the need for teachers who are well prepared to support learners with varying needs and levels of skill, TEPs need to provide opportunities for PSTs to see differentiation in action and understand how to apply it to their future practice, and teacher educators need to understand and leverage their own position as role models for the PSTs in their courses (Gheyssens et al., 2020). TEPs are often the first opportunity for PSTs to engage in structured and supported practice in applying teaching approaches such as differentiation (De Neve & Devos, 2015). In order to support PST understanding of DI, teacher educators should model such practices in their own teaching (Gaitas & Martins, 2017; Scarparolo & Subban, 2021) and be explicit in how and why DI is being used (Scarparolo & Subban, 2021). Opportunities to learn strategies for differentiation and reflect on the use of DI result in PSTs who feel better prepared to support diverse learners and have more positive attitudes about the use of DI (De Neve & Devos, 2015). It is of note that in a survey of TEP instructors in the United States, 95 percent responded that they differentiate process within their courses, while just over 56 percent indicated that they differentiate by product (Lockley et al., 2017). However, additional research in international contexts indicates that many teacher educators lack training in DI themselves, making it difficult for them to model and enact it within their own classrooms (Zelalem et al., 2022). Considering the lack of knowledge of some teacher educators, as well as the fact that PSTs still feel unprepared to enact DI in their future classrooms (Scarparolo & Subban, 2021), more explicit and purposeful work is needed to support understanding and application of DI principles within TEPs.

As is true in pre-K–12 education, the use of DI in teacher education can also provide opportunities to support the learning needs of diverse PSTs while also providing the benefits of effective modeling of this pedagogical approach that PSTs can carry forward into their own practice (Dack, 2018). This has also been supported by limited research regarding the positive impact of DI within TEPs (Joseph et al., 2013) and in higher education more generally (Chamberlin & Powers, 2010; Jørgensen & Brogaard, 2021; Santangelo & Tomlinson, 2009). However, more research into the use of specific strategies for differentiating instruction in teacher education and higher education is needed, as much of what is currently available perpetuates misconceptions, such as those related to learning styles.

Explicit Modeling of DI in Teacher Education

Modeling of practice and pedagogy within TEPs is a practice viewed as important to supporting the development of effective teachers (Moore & Bell, 2019). Modeling, particularly explicit modeling, in which the strategies or tools being used are clearly identified to PSTs, is a valuable practice within TEPs where it helps PSTs bridge the gap between theory and practice (Moore & Bell, 2019). Teacher educators serve the dual role of supporting PSTs' understanding of teaching while also modeling the role of the teacher (Lunenberg et al., 2007). Failure to consciously model best practices within TEPs results in a missed opportunity to break the cycle of the apprenticeship of observation (Lortie, 1975). Thus, it is vital that schools of education approach teacher education as a setting for rich, reflective, professional development (Ball & Cohen, 1999). However, explicit modeling is complex, and supports are needed to integrate explicit modeling effectively into teacher educators' practice (Loughram & Berry, 2005; Scarparolo & Subban, 2021). Previous research has indicated that the use of pedagogical tools such as DI must be explicitly identified and the instructor's decision-making processes connected to theory for PSTs to identify these tools as elements experienced within their own coursework (Dack, 2018).

Opportunities to experience strategies for differentiation and reflect on the use of DI can result in PSTs who feel better prepared to support diverse learners, have more positive attitudes about the use of DI (De Neve & Devos, 2015), and carry fewer misconceptions regarding differentiation (Dack, 2018). In addition, purposeful integration of DI across coursework, assignments, and clinical placements can help PSTs develop a more nuanced understanding of how to tailor instruction based on learners' varied needs.

Challenges to Enacting Differentiation in Higher Education

Higher-education programs, including TEPs, are a context that poses unique challenges to enacting differentiation in comparison to typical pre-K–12 education programs. Among these are the lack of stable and dedicated classroom space and the reduced amount of time instructors in TEPs have to engage students within the classroom. Additional challenges noted by TEP instructors are class sizes, inflexible curricula, and the need for additional support in enacting DI (Lockley et al., 2017).

Students in K–12 classrooms attend school for between 200 and 630 hours per semester (Silva-Padron & McCann, 2023). In high school, students spend approximately 30 hours per week in classes, whereas full-time students in college spend 12 to 16 hours per week in classes (Kings College, 2023). Thus, instructors at the college level have a more limited amount of time in class to engage with and get to know the students in their courses (Lockley et al., 2017), limiting their ability to use knowledge of student strengths and interests in purposeful planning of DI.

Unlike most teachers in K–12 classrooms, instructors at the higher-education level often lack a dedicated teaching space. Classrooms in higher education tend to be shared spaces, and a specific class may or may not be scheduled in the same classroom from one semester to the next. This makes it more difficult to utilize strategies, such as different configurations of student seating. In addition, the short time between courses in a specific space (often 10 to 15 minutes) limits instructors' ability to engage students with activities that may require extensive setup and cleanup.

Overcoming the Challenges to Move to Enactment and Reflection: About This Book

It is my hope that this book will serve as a tool to support teacher educators in their enactment of DI while also providing both the teacher educator and their PSTs with opportunities for impactful reflection on the strategies implemented. With this in mind, I have filled each chapter with specific strategies, tools, and examples from a variety of content areas relevant to teacher education. In addition, each chapter includes reflection questions for both the teacher educator and PSTs to help them consider the effectiveness and impact of the DI strategies and tools being modeled within the TEP and, for PSTs, consider how they may implement these in their future classrooms to support diverse student needs. The inclusion of questions for TEP faculty not only engages them in purposefully considering the strategies they are choosing to implement but also provides opportunities for faculty to model the thought process and dispositions of a reflective practitioner.

Chapter 1 focuses on how to introduce the differentiated classroom to PSTs, the importance of explicit modeling as a teacher educator, and how to approach reflection for PSTs using the Dual Role Reflection Model, which acknowledges the two roles in which PSTs find themselves during their TEP: learner and educator in training.

Chapter 2 zooms in on the importance of assessment in implementing DI effectively. The chapter includes a variety of tools for pre-assessment of PST knowledge, skills, and attitudes as well as assessments for use during and after instruction to gauge PST growth and identify any remaining questions or misconceptions. The chapter also provides examples of how to differentiate content, process, and product based on assessment results.

Chapter 3 discusses differentiation by environment, including specific strategies for both in-person and virtual classes to create a classroom environment in which PSTs feel valued, are comfortable taking risks, and are part of a community of learners. This includes strategies to set a positive and welcoming tone from the initial meeting, strategies to encourage students to interact positively with a variety of peers, and tools for inviting student feedback within the course.

Chapter 4 focuses on content differentiation, including differentiation of materials and of instructional supports. This chapter builds on Chapter

2 by providing strategies to support PSTs who need more support and engagement with foundational information based on assessment results while also providing opportunities for PSTs who have grasped foundational information and skills to engage in higher-order application and analysis.

Chapter 5 provides strategies and tools for differentiating by process, which involves varying how students engage with course materials based on their learning needs, background knowledge, and current level of proficiency. This chapter includes general strategies to support PST success as well as strategies and tools for adjusting the complexity of tasks and for providing PSTs with various levels of scaffolding.

Chapter 6 discusses differentiation by product, which varies how students demonstrate their learning and growth. This chapter provides examples of choice boards; suggestions for products in multiple modalities that PSTs can create to demonstrate their knowledge, skills, and ability to connect theory to practice; and example rubrics for use with differentiated products.

Chapter 7 focuses on the importance of implementing DI across the TEP, pushing teacher educators and PSTs to consider how integration of DI across courses can more effectively support PST understanding and the future application of DI principles in their future classrooms. Strategies for implementation across the TEP, including ideas for faculty development and collaboration with colleagues within the program and from partner K–12 schools, are discussed.

1 Introducing the Differentiated Classroom to Your Preservice Teachers

I had never seen differentiation so laid out before. It was really helpful.
—Preservice teacher in K–8 ELA methods, spring 2018

Each semester as a new class of preservice teachers (PSTs) makes their way into my classroom, I start with activities that let me get to know their experiences as learners and their attitudes toward the course content area, such as peer interviews (see Chapter 3 for activity ideas). Within my teacher education program (TEP), I primarily teach courses focused on English language arts. Through these activities, a set of themes typically emerges as PSTs share their learning experiences, with few differences from one semester to the next: standardized testing, reading for points, and memorable assignments that involved choice and interest. The first two tend to be met with communal groans from the PSTs in the course, while the last are shared with excitement and fondness. These different responses provide opportunities for reflecting on what made these experiences memorable (for good or ill) and open the door for discussion regarding many topics related to utilizing differentiated instruction (DI). This conversation also serves as a transition to discussing the current course, including expectations and assignments.

This is my first opportunity to introduce the concept of differentiation to PSTs in the course. We discuss the differences that are evident (and those that may be hidden) among the many students in a single class, whether they are in pre-K–12 or college.

What Is the Difference Between Equal and Equitable?

This is a discussion that PSTs may engage in multiple times during their TEP, as it is relevant and, for some, will take multiple opportunities to truly "get" it. There are popular images that provide visuals to support understanding of these concepts, ranging from children trying to watch a sports event from behind a fence to people of various heights and abilities choosing a bicycle to ride. I ask students to search for an image that best represents their understanding of equity and put it into a sharable digital space (such as a shared online Web page in the learning management system or in another tool, such as a Padlet). We then take time to discuss the definition of each term (equality meaning that each person gets the same resources or opportunities; equity meaning that each person gets the resources and opportunities they need to reach the intended outcome) and the images they selected. To guide discussion of the images, I ask PSTs to consider the following:

- What message is the image sending about equal and equitable?
- Who is included, and who might be missing from the image?
- Does the image fully capture the complexity of equity in education?

I follow up with the following series of prompts to engage students in reflecting on their own experiences as learners.

Not Everyone Needs the Same Amount of Time to Complete a Task

I ask my students to think about a time when they felt they had to put in more time and effort to achieve the same level of success or completion in comparison to their peers. It doesn't have to be something academic; it can be learning a new sport like skiing or learning how to play an instrument. Would they have been successful if they had been limited to the same amount of time to succeed as the person who finished or reached proficiency first? What did the person who achieved success earlier do once they had reached proficiency? This discussion leads to topics such as providing enrichment and challenge for students who meet a standard or learning goal quickly while also providing the structure and support for students who need more time to achieve proficiency.

Not Everyone Comes in with the Same Background Knowledge and Experiences

One of my favorite stories to share with my PSTs is the tale of the Florida camel ride writing prompt. In 2012, the timed writing prompt for the fourth-grade standardized writing assessment asked students across the state of Florida to write a story about a camel ride, complete with relevant and logical support. Naturally, most students had never ridden on a camel and had no real idea of what might happen on a camel ride. Scores that year were significantly lower than expected, and, while the prompt wasn't the only factor (a tougher grading rubric had also been used that accounted for spelling, grammar, and mechanics to a higher degree than previous years; Boyd, 2012; Samples, 2012), my fourth-grade teacher colleagues were frustrated and aimed much of that frustration at the prompt. Students simply did not have the background knowledge to respond confidently. To many, it felt more like a test of background knowledge and/or imagination than one of writing skill.

Now imagine, I tell my PSTs, that everyone else has the background knowledge to respond to the prompt. Perhaps they went on a class trip to the zoo the previous year and all of them got to ride a camel—everyone except you because you just moved to the area. How do you feel facing that timed writing prompt? Do you feel confident in your ability to show your writing skill? Has there been a time in your educational journey when you were being asked to engage in a task for which you needed additional background knowledge to be successful? How did that impact your confidence in completing the task? Why do these feelings matter?

Not Everyone Has the Same Strengths (Artistic, Athletic, and Academic Subjects)

I share my own strengths, as well as the areas in which I am less skilled, with the PSTs in my courses. For example, while I am a strong writer, I am a mediocre (at best) visual artist. Thus, when given a choice between creating a written product or an artistic visualization, I am typically going to choose the written product because I feel more confident that I will be able to communicate effectively in that format. Does that mean I should never draw? Of course not! (Well, according to some of my previous middle school students, it might!) But it does make me consider, in my role as an educator, what modalities or approaches to developing and sharing knowledge and skill are appropriate to the content and standards being covered while still leveraging student strengths when possible. If the goal of an assignment is to gauge the ability to write in complete sentences, then a written product will be needed, although this product could include a variety of formats (traditional paper, presentation, website, blog, and so on). If the goal is to analyze a short video of a classroom to identify best practices being utilized, then this could be done through a variety of modalities ranging from a written product to a conversation between the PST and instructor. Some tasks will be opportunities to strengthen skills or knowledge through modalities, content, or approaches that the individual is not as strong or confident in, while others will be opportunities to engage their strengths. DI provides a framework for teachers to balance these opportunities thoughtfully while keeping the standards, goals, or objectives students are working toward in the forefront.

Within the discussions about the points above, I ask the PSTs in my class to consider and share the following:

- How have their teachers balanced these issues (equitable instruction and assessment, adjusting to meet student needs in terms of time to reach proficiency, background knowledge, and student strengths) in the past?
- Did the strategies they encountered as students feel effective for supporting their learning?
- Did the strategies they encountered feel equitable for all students in the classroom?
- What challenges might teachers face as they work to create equity in their own classrooms?

During the discussion, I share my own experiences as both a learner and an educator.

When I worked as a middle and high school language arts teacher, I found that many of the students who struggled in my classes were no less capable than their peers; they simply needed a different means with which to access content or express their knowledge and learning than the methods I mainly depended on: multiple-choice tests and written responses, such as essays. Although I made accommodations for students whose individualized education programs (IEPs) required them, it took time for me to understand that all the students in my class could benefit from instructional and assessment opportunities that let them play to their strengths and provide scaffolds and supports for the areas in which they were (or felt) less successful.

As a student, I was a quick finisher of most class assignments. Few of my teachers provided enrichment opportunities or differentiated work to challenge me and either left me to read on my own when I was finished or asked me to assist peers who needed additional support. These experiences left me frustrated and feeling like an afterthought in many of my classes over the years. When I began my teaching career, these experiences shaped how I approached my instruction. In addition to making sure I support all students in successfully meeting the appropriate standards or proficiencies, I also make it a point not to hold any students back from accomplishing the level of skill, knowledge, or application they are capable of. One eighth-grade student I worked with sticks out in my mind—this student entered my class with broad background knowledge and strong comprehension. The student also started each year very oppositional to teachers. This opposition could be overcome in one of two ways: by showing the student you had something to offer them in terms of knowledge or skills or by asking the student what they wanted to learn for any given unit. I took the second approach. When my class began reading and analyzing a novel that the student had already read multiple times on their own, I asked if there were other books by that author that were of interest. They quickly identified one. Throughout the unit, this student did activities focused on the same literary elements and critical thinking skills as the rest of the class while using a different text.

I continue our discussion by identifying misconceptions the PSTs may have regarding DI. Many PSTs initially view DI as an overwhelming task, believing that it requires completely individualized lesson plans for every student. In addition to those discussed in the introduction of this book, we also discuss DI as a practice focused on meeting the needs of all learners, not just those who need additional support. This includes dispelling the myth that differentiation is solely for struggling students, reinforcing that it is equally essential for students who excel and would benefit from enrichment opportunities. This includes opportunities to provide enrichment for students who have shown proficiency in content and to provide alternative ways to access content for students who have learning differences. By framing differentiation as a means to honor the full spectrum of student abilities, we help PSTs understand that it enhances learning for everyone, not just those who need intervention.

We then discuss the importance of providing students with the access and opportunities they need to reach their fullest potential. This involves ensuring that all students are appropriately challenged and engaged rather than simply completing tasks at their current level of proficiency. To deepen their understanding, we also explore how differentiation is not about creating entirely separate lessons for each student but about using flexible strategies to accommodate diverse learning needs within a shared classroom environment. I emphasize that differentiation can take many forms, including adjusting content complexity, modifying instructional strategies, and offering multiple ways for students to demonstrate their learning. By embracing a flexible and responsive approach, teachers can create inclusive learning experiences that support all students in reaching their highest potential.

In looking over the syllabus, many PSTs in my courses have questions regarding the open-ended choice assignments (see examples in Chapter 6). While some are excited about the choice of products or approaches available in these tasks (Subban et al., 2024), others express discomfort with the options available, as they are more used to heavily proscribed course tasks that do not provide a great deal of freedom in terms of format, topic, and so on. Some also indicate they are overwhelmed by the choices available. In addition, open-ended assignments require students to be more self-directed in their learning, which can be challenging for some students without sufficient scaffolds. To support my PSTs as they engage in open-ended tasks within a DI framework, I provide structure through menu projects tied clearly to course learning outcomes that have incremental deadlines throughout the semester (see Chapter 6 for more details). I also provide models of the tasks so that PSTs can see examples of successful products.

Supporting PST Understanding of Differentiation

Striving for Relevance

Within a differentiated classroom, regardless of the students' grade level or age, there are opportunities for students to be challenged and engage in higher-order thinking. However, it is important that students don't just see these opportunities as busywork or, even worse, a punishment for "getting it." When students perceive advanced tasks as tedious or disconnected from their interests, they may disengage rather than embrace the challenge. One of the most important things I consider when engaging the students who are ready to dig deeper into the content is how to make the content, process, or product relevant to their lives, goals, or interests. Relevance fosters intrinsic motivation, making learning feel purposeful rather than obligatory. Sometimes this involves compacting my curriculum, which allows students to skip activities that are meant to reinforce or practice skills or knowledge not yet mastered. This ensures that they spend their time on meaningful exploration rather than unnecessary repetition. In some cases, this is as simple as asking, "What else do you want to know?" or "How would you like to apply what you have learned?" Often, the response to these questions is something I would not have thought of myself and provides a foundation for alternative product options or extension activities as well as deeper learning that is supported by student buy-in. By giving PSTs a voice in how they extend their learning, I empower them to take ownership of their education, leading to greater engagement and more authentic learning experiences.

Explicit Modeling as a Teacher Educator

As I engage in DI and other best practices within my instruction, I endeavor to be explicit in what I am modeling and why I am utilizing a specific approach or strategy. I also try to model the parts of instructional practice that may feel hidden, such as planning for instruction. For example, at the beginning of each class meeting, I share an agenda that includes the topic(s) we will be focused on, the relevant course learning outcome(s), and how PSTs will be assessed on each learning outcome (formative and/or summative). As I introduce the agenda the first couple of times, I share how I employed backward design in creating the course and how the course learning outcomes serve in place of standards to identify what the PSTs should know and be able to do by the end of the course. This agenda also provides the PSTs with clear expectations for each class meeting as well as long-term expectations through the summative assessments connected to each learning outcome.

I follow this process with assigned tasks in class as well, providing an explicit rationale for the task and connecting it to the relevant course outcome(s). For example, in a literacy assessment course that I have taught, the PSTs tutor a local student over the course of the semester using data from a variety of assessments administered to identify student strengths and needs and tailor their instruction. As part of the course, PSTs write a letter to their students' caregivers to share what they have learned about the student's literacy strengths and areas for growth as well as to provide suggestions for activities to support the student's literacy development at home. As I assign this task to PSTs in the course, I share the following rationale: The goal of this activity is to provide you with a scaffolded opportunity to practice communicating with caregivers about their child's literacy progress. Before you share this letter with your students' caregivers, I will read your draft and provide feedback and suggestions to help you communicate with your students' caregivers using strengths-based and growth-oriented language.

Another element of the differentiated classroom that requires explicit modeling for PSTs in my courses is the use of clear expectations to support student independence and the level of autonomy they will experience as they engage with specific tools for differentiation, such as choice projects (Chapter 6), task charts (Chapter 4), or learning contracts (Chapter 4). Establishing clear expectations includes providing learning targets that make explicit what PSTs should know or be able to do after engaging with content and providing explicit guidelines for what success looks like as they demonstrate their new knowledge or skills. This last part can include examples from previous semesters (anonymized and/or shared with permission of the creator) and instructor-created models.

Reflecting as a Teacher Educator

One of my goals as a teacher educator is to model for the PSTs in my courses the process of continuously refining my practice as an educator. Reflection is an important tool for supporting PSTs in developing their professional identities (Szocik et al., 2021) and helping them apply their developing knowledge and skills to problems of practice. Among the strategies I use for this are explicitly eliciting and responding to PST feedback throughout the semester (see Chapter 3 for discussion and activities to support this) and sharing my own reflections on course activities and assignments, including what I will do differently or keep the same the next time I utilize them. This requires a level of humility and vulnerability that can be difficult. However, I have found that being transparent in my reflection (Beauchamp, 2014) and identifying what I plan to adjust in future iterations of instruction is well received by PSTs, who comment that it provides a model-in-practice of being a reflective educator.

Opportunities for Reflecting on DI in Teacher Education

Reflection is viewed as an important step in the professionalization of students in TEPs (Miller et al., 2021). PSTs within TEPs are frequently asked to reflect on their experiences, their own instruction within field placements, and how they (will and/or do) apply theory to practice. Indeed, reflection for PSTs is an opportunity for continued professional growth through critical analysis of their experiences, memories, instructional choices, and biases (Hong et al., 2022). However, current models of reflection focus on the process of reflection itself (e.g., Gibbs, 1988; Kolb, 1984) or the expected dimension or nature of reflection (e.g., Hatton & Smith, 1995; Ward & McCotter, 2004) and do not acknowledge the dual role that PSTs are navigating within their TEPs. They are learners who are engaging in coursework to develop the knowledge and skills required for their profession *and* are educators-in-training who are considering the practical application of their new knowledge and skills to their future (and in some cases current) classrooms. Thus, they need to be able to reflect in both these roles. Indeed, their experiences and interactions as learners within their initial education as well as in their higher-education courses often influence their own teaching (Lortie, 1975). In addition, as PSTs progress through their program, they are expected to transition to more of an educator mindset and reflect in accordance with this role. With these dual roles and the expected transition into thinking and reflecting like an educator in addition to reflecting as a learner, it may be necessary to provide scaffolding and connections between the two roles to support PSTs in engaging in levels of reflection appropriate to a novice educator (deBettencourt & Nagro, 2018). Indeed, supporting the transition from reflecting as learners to reflecting as an educator is even more imperative given the current trend in many areas of the United States of PSTs serving as a teacher-of-record with a professional contract or as a long-term substitute during their student teaching semester due to a shortage of already licensed educators (Massachusetts Department of Elementary & Secondary Education, 2023; Missouri State University, 2024; South Dakota Legislature, 2023).

Research indicates that PSTs' reflections tend to focus on themselves as opposed to their students and classroom contexts regardless of where they are within their clinical experiences (deBettencourt & Nagro, 2018), and they tend to treat reflective writing assignments as more of a descriptive task than one of analysis and higher-level thinking (Jones & Ryan, 2014; Yee et al., 2022). This tendency can limit the depth and effectiveness of reflection, as focusing mainly on oneself limits perspective taking and obscures insights regarding student learning, classroom discourse, and dynamics. By acknowledging that reflection is a social practice (Beauchamp, 2014; Zeichner & Liu, 2010) and providing opportunities for PSTs to reflect with their peers and support one another's growth, teacher educators can support richer reflection that incorporates multiple perspectives for their PSTs and that also considers issues of equity and justice within their practice. However, it is also important that PSTs are provided explicit instruction and support to engage in collegial and valuable peer feedback (Erdemire & Yeşilçınar, 2021).

It is also important to consider that reflection is appropriate not only for PSTs in a field experience. Even those not engaged in a clinical experience can engage in reflective practice to consider connections between the skills, knowledge, and theory they are learning and their classroom practice (Nelson et al., 2016). This may also include reflecting on the strategies and skills they observe being utilized within the TEP classroom. However, reflecting within this specific context requires teacher educators to be purposeful and explicit in the utilization of the best practices they teach PSTs and to serve as models of what these practices look like when enacted.

Research also indicates encouraging PSTs to reflect on professional dispositions (Szocik et al., 2021), and their own positionality within teaching practicums (Zhu & Chen, 2022) can support the development of professional identity. Purposeful reflection on professional identity and the dispositions and skills that are part of that identity can support PSTs in examining their own positionality and in critically analyzing how their backgrounds and experiences influence their beliefs and practices as an educator.

With that in mind, I have developed a Dual Role Reflection Model (Figure 1) that considers the two roles of PSTs within the TEP (learner and educator-in-training) in tandem for PSTs engaged in reflection on the instruction they are experiencing within their courses, the instruction they have seen and are seeing enacted within pre-K–12 classrooms, and the instruction they are delivering within their field experiences. Within each role, there are three lenses through which PSTs reflect, with each lens within the learner role having a parallel lens within the educator role. This model asks PSTs to consider their experiences from these lenses as a learner: their own personal lens, a lens that is informed by the experiences of their peers, and a third lens that asks them to purposefully consider how their instructor is using knowledge and strategies to support learner success. From the perspective of an educator-in-training, the framework mirrors these levels, pushing PSTs to apply what they experience to their future classroom by considering the application of these experiences to their own content (grade range and/or content area), the learners in their future classroom, and their own instruction. Between these two levels are bridges that identify guiding statements for supporting PSTs as they transition from the learner role to the educator-in-training role.

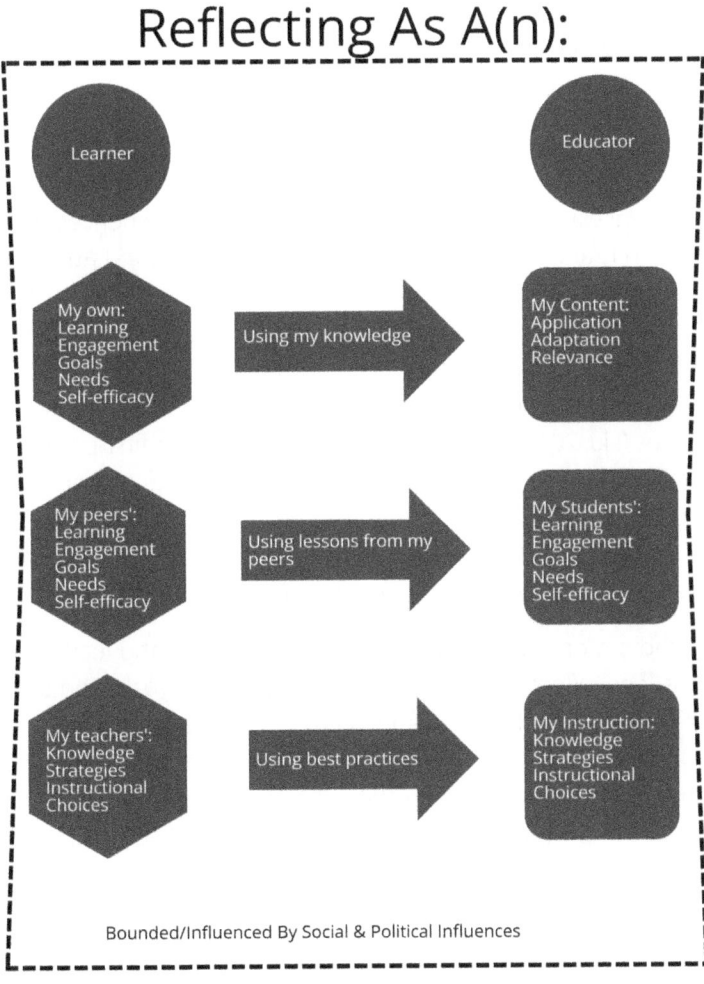

Figure 1 Dual Role Reflection Model.

Each set of lenses in the Dual Role Reflection Model progresses from the easiest for PSTs to utilize to the most difficult based on previous research into PST reflection (deBettencourt & Nagro, 2018). This model also provides opportunities for PSTs to reflect both retrospectively (reflecting on past experiences) and prospectively (reflecting on application in their current and future classrooms), thus addressing a common critique of many models of reflection as only backward facing (Conway, 2001). Each pair of lenses will be discussed in detail below. Note that since social and political influences on teaching and learning (Liu, 2015) need to be considered in both roles and through all perspectives, the model includes these influences as bounding all other elements within the model to visually denote the ubiquitousness of these influences. Each set of lenses needs to be considered together with the bridging statement in order to avoid continuation of the either/or reflection binary this model seeks to address.

The first set of lenses is the "in my experience" lens. Through their lens as learners, PSTs reflect on themselves, including their learning (both knowledge and experiences), their engagement in learning experiences, their goals within the TEP, and their own self-efficacy as learners. PSTs using this lens should also consider how their own background and culture shape how they view the various elements of their educational experience in order to identify, address, and challenge their own biases. Additionally, PSTs should consider the social and political pressures that influenced their educational experiences (Liu, 2015). Within the role of educator, this first-person lens asks PSTs to reflect on their own application and adaptation of content within their teaching (including teaching within the TEP classroom and field experience classroom). This includes considering how social and political pressures will/do influence how they teach their content (Liu, 2015).

The second set of lenses is the "in the desks" lens. In the learner role, PSTs using this lens reflect on the learning, engagement, goals, and self-efficacy of their peers (both their peers in pre-K–12 education and their peers in the TEP) as well as how their peers' background and culture serve as lenses through which their peers view the various elements of their experience. This requires opportunities for PSTs to discuss and reflect collaboratively on their past educational experiences as well as their experiences within the TEP and their clinical placements. Shifting to this lens within the educator role pushes PSTs to consider how they (can/will) apply and adapt what they have learned within the TEP to meet the needs of diverse learners through their teaching (including teaching within the TEP classroom and field experience classroom) and how their ability to meet these needs may be influenced by outside pressures and influences (Liu, 2015). This includes consideration of their students' learning, engagement, goals, needs, and self-efficacy as learners within the classroom and school context.

The final set of lenses is the "in the profession" lens. In the learner role, PSTs utilizing this lens are reflecting on the knowledge and strategies being utilized/modeled and the instructional choices made by their course instructors and the teachers within their field placements as well as how these strategies may be informed by the teachers' knowledge of best practices, their students' needs, and political and social pressures and norms (Liu, 2015). In the educator role, PSTs are reflecting on their own (current/future) use of instructional strategies in the same way.

Between each set of lenses is a "bridge" that provides a scaffolding statement connecting the lens in the learner role to its companion in the educator role. Each bridge provides a guiding action statement to help the PST consider how to shift from the learner role to the educator role. This bridge focuses on a key element that ties the two lenses together, serving as a foundation for transitioning between the two roles.

Between the "in my experience" lenses, the connecting statement is "Using my knowledge." This statement reminds PSTs that their reflections through this lens will be focused on themselves—their knowledge as informed by their learning and experiences. Thus, within both roles, this will likely be the easiest reflective lens for PSTs to utilize, as research indicates that PSTs tend to be more successful in reflecting at a personal level (deBettencourt & Nagro, 2018). Thus, PSTs transitioning from the learner to the educator role through this lens may be considering how their own experiences as a student shape their beliefs about teaching their own content and the ways in which these beliefs have shifted during their experiences in the TEP. Based on this, what will/does instruction in their classroom look like?

Between the "in the desk" lenses, the connecting statement is "Using lessons from my peers." This statement pushes PSTs to consider what they have learned from the experiences of their peers and apply that understanding to meeting the needs of the students within their own classroom(s). With this in mind, PSTs transitioning from the learner to the educator role through the "in the desk" lens may be considering how their own biases impact their ability

Table 1 Example Reflection Graphic Organizer

Reflection prompt: How does the course instructor communicate the learning objectives for the course to you, as a student? How does this impact your approach to the course?

Perspective		As a Learner		As an Educator
In my experience	Considering my own learning, engagement, needs, goals, and self-efficacy	In this course, my instructor shares the learning objectives in the syllabus and also connects them to what we do in each class meeting. When the instructor clearly communicates learning objectives, I feel more engaged and confident in my learning. I can set personal goals, monitor progress, and connect content to my goals. When objectives are unclear, I may feel uncertain about expectations or disengaged.	Considering my application and adaptation of content and its relevance	Communicating clear learning objectives helps students see the purpose behind their work, potentially increasing motivation and self-efficacy. I strive to make objectives explicit, relevant, and accessible to diverse learners through multiple formats like I have observed in my field placement.
In the desks	Considering my peers' learning, engagement, needs, goals, and self-efficacy	My peers benefit from clear objectives because they create a shared understanding of expectations. This clarity enhances collaboration, discussion, and collective engagement with course content. When objectives are vague, students may struggle with direction and feel disconnected from learning.	Considering my students' learning, engagement, needs, goals, and self-efficacy	I consider how my students process and engage with learning objectives. Ensuring clarity through scaffolding, visuals, and real-world applications supports students with varying needs and backgrounds. When students understand the "why" behind their learning, they engage more meaningfully.

In the profession	Considering my teacher's knowledge, strategies, and instructional choices	My instructor's ability to communicate objectives through explicit explanations, modeling, and connections to professional contexts shapes my perception of effective teaching. I notice how different strategies influence my motivation and ability to apply knowledge.	Considering my pedagogical knowledge, strategies, and instructional choices	I refine my instructional choices by ensuring that learning objectives are student-centered, measurable, and relevant. Drawing from my experiences as a learner, I use clear communication, structured guidance, and reflective opportunities to enhance student understanding and engagement.

Final synthesis question: How do your experiences as a learner influence your approach as an educator, and how might my understanding as an educator reshape the way you engage with learning in the future? What insights from both roles can you apply to better support diverse learners in my classroom?

Response: My experiences as a learner show me that clear, well-communicated learning outcomes make a significant difference in engagement and success. When instructors clearly define and share course objectives, I feel more motivated, focused, and confident in my learning. As an educator, this understanding shapes my approach—I prioritize making learning goals explicit, relevant, and accessible through multiple formats to support diverse learners.

Being an educator also changes how I approach learning. I've realized that when I understand why I'm learning something and how it connects to real life, I stay more engaged and motivated. Now, I try to be more proactive in asking questions, making connections, and using feedback to improve. By looking at both perspectives, I can create a classroom where all students understand what's expected, see the value in what they're learning, and feel more confident in their abilities.

to meet the needs of their students and building on the shared experiences of their peers to push themselves to consider the perspectives of the diverse students within their classroom.

The "in the profession" lens is connected by the statement "Using best practices." The goal of this statement is to remind PSTs that good instruction is guided by practices based on sound research, to push them to use that knowledge of best practices to identify them within the models they have experienced, and to apply them to their own teaching. PSTs transitioning from the learner to the educator role may be considering their own lessons or lesson plans and reflecting on the strategies and tools included, their reasons for including those specific strategies and tools, and how to pivot if the selected strategies prove to be ineffective for their specific students or context.

It is important to note that while each of the three levels is distinct, they can be integrated to further scaffold the reflection process for PSTs. Ideally, PSTs will be able to connect their reflections across the three sets of lenses in order to critically examine their own instruction, its impact on the students in their classrooms, and how their own experiences and biases have shaped their beliefs and practice as an educator. For some PSTs who will benefit from a more structured approach for digging into reflection questions, I have also used a graphic organizer (Table 1). For a blank version of this graphic organizer that can help PSTs consider both roles as they engage in reflection questions, see Appendix A.

Reflection and Discussion Questions

"As a Teacher Educator" reflection questions are for the course instructor to reflect on their utilization of DI. "As a Learner" and "As an Educator" questions are for PSTs to reflect on their experience with differentiation as a learner and to consider how they can apply that experience and their new knowledge to their future classrooms. These two sets of questions consider the dual roles of PSTs in the TEP. It is recommended that PSTs have an opportunity to reflect on these questions individually before sharing and discussing them with peers.

As a Teacher Educator:

1 How have your personal experiences as a learner shaped the way you approach teaching and differentiation in your courses?
2 How do you introduce DI to your PSTs?

3   Are the learning objectives for the course explicitly communicated to the students in the course? Are these learning objectives explicitly tied to the content and tasks within the course?
4   Are you aware of the various cultural backgrounds of the PSTs in the course? Have you considered how to use this knowledge to increase the relevance of the materials and take advantage of the knowledge they bring to the course?
5   How do you scaffold discussions that help PSTs think critically about what equitable instruction looks like in practice?
6   How do you explicitly model best practices for differentiation in your own instruction, and how do you ensure that PSTs can apply these practices in their future classrooms?
7   How do you model planning practices like backward design, and how do you communicate the value of these practices to your PSTs?
8   In what ways do you model reflective practice for your students? How do you demonstrate vulnerability in this process?

As a Learner:

1   How does the course instructor communicate the learning objectives for the course to you, as a student? How does this impact your approach to the course?
2   How does knowledge of the course learning objectives support you as a student? Consider issues such as relevance and importance of the material, goal setting, and connections to past or future coursework.
3   Can you recall a situation in your education (in K–12 or in college) where you felt the need for more time, support, or a different approach to help you understand something? How did your teacher respond to those needs?
4   Recall a time when you struggled with a task or assignment due to a lack of background knowledge. How did it affect your confidence? How might your teacher have helped bridge that gap for you?
5   How did your past teachers handle DI, and how did it impact your learning?
6   Reflect on a classroom where you felt that instruction or assessment was either equitable or inequitable. What made it feel that way? How did the students (yourself and your peers) respond in this context?

7 In what ways do you see your instructor utilizing knowledge of students' cultural backgrounds to increase the relevance of materials and to provide students with opportunities to connect their existing knowledge to new learning?

As an Educator:

1 What does it mean to create an equitable classroom? What do you think might be some common misconceptions about equity in education?

2 Consider the developmental level of the students you will be or are working with. How can you communicate learning objectives for lessons in a way that is developmentally appropriate for these students?

3 How might you support a student who lacks the necessary background knowledge for an assignment? How can you ensure that all students are prepared to succeed regardless of their prior experiences?

4 What strategies will you use to create a classroom culture where students see differentiated tasks and activities as opportunities for growth rather than as punishment or busywork?

5 As a future educator, how do you envision balancing support for struggling students while also challenging students who are ready to extend their learning?

6 How have your instructors in your TEP and/or the teachers you have observed in your field experiences modeled instructional strategies, such as differentiation or backward design? Are there strategies you have seen modeled that you want to implement in your own teaching?

7 How might you work with your future colleagues to implement differentiated strategies in a cohesive way?

8 How do you perceive the role of reflection in your development as an educator? How do you plan to incorporate reflection into your own practice?

2 How Assessment Supports Differentiated Instruction

Assessment is a tool utilized to determine where a student is in their learning (Westman, 2018). Both formative (assessment for purposes of improving student learning through adjustments to future instruction and/or to identify areas of difficulty for students) and summative (assessment to determine how much a student knows, has retained, or can engage in a specific skill) assessments provide opportunities for teachers to gauge student learning and plan for future instruction (Dixson & Worrell, 2016). Assessments can take a variety of forms, depending on the purpose of the assessment. Formative assessments, which are generally intended to provide data to adjust instruction and support student learning, can include homework or in-class assignments, teacher observations during instruction and classroom discussion, and student self-evaluations and reflections. Summative assessments, typically utilized to evaluate student learning outcomes, may include traditional tests, projects, performance assessments, and essays or other written products (Dixson & Worrell, 2016). Recent research indicates secondary teachers (grades 6–12) tend to use questioning strategies, homework, and teacher-created tests as their most utilized forms of assessment (Wherfel et al., 2022) for both general and special education students. Additionally, research shows that high school teachers tend to provide higher levels of individualized formative feedback in response to assessments than teachers at other levels in K–12 education (Johnson et al., 2019).

However, research has found that novice teachers often indicate low levels of knowledge and skills related to assessment (Atjonen et al., 2022). Additional research suggests that recent graduates and current students within initial teacher licensure programs indicate little experience with formative assessments specifically (Hamodi et al., 2017; Starck et al., 2023). Despite this lack of experience with formative assessments, recent graduates viewed formative assessments positively (Hamodi et al., 2017) and expressed a desire to utilize formative assessments within their own practice (Atjonen et al., 2022; Starck et al., 2023). Furthermore, those who indicated that they had experienced formative assessments specifically were able to clearly delineate the differences between grading and assessment (Hamodi et al., 2017) and demonstrated teaching competencies related to assessment (Cañadas, 2023). Recent graduates also indicate that transparency regarding the specific learning objectives they were assessed on during their TEP supported their own learning by indicating what they should focus on in their studies (Cañadas, 2023). Given the findings of recent research regarding teachers' implementation of formative assessment that indicate that teacher self-efficacy and prior training in utilizing assessment are factors contributing to their use of formative assessment (Yan et al., 2021), training and professional development are needed to support the understanding and application of assessment by preservice teachers (PSTs), particularly of assessment for purposes of identifying student growth fairly and using that information to inform instruction (Oo et al., 2023). Additional research indicates that PSTs value authentic assessment methods (Brunker et al., 2019) that both challenge them to apply their knowledge and help them consider how to utilize these assessments in their own practice. This speaks to the importance of purposeful and transparent inclusion of best practices for formative assessment within TEPs along with opportunities for PSTs to reflect on these practices.

In addition, PSTs may view assessment as separate from teaching, as opposed to related to or informing teaching and may lack confidence in their ability to effectively use assessment (Starck et al., 2023). Without a strong understanding of how assessment can guide instruction, PSTs may struggle to use assessment data in meaningful ways, leading to missed opportunities for responsive teaching that meets the diverse needs of students. This can include opportunities within their field placements and in their coursework. For example, I have shared overall results of course assessments with PSTs in my courses and discussed the patterns evident in the class's performance. By engaging PSTs in the results of their own course's assessment data, I am able to model data-driven decision-making and make my own decisions as an instructor transparent.

While PSTs in field placements may have opportunities to discuss utilizing assessment to inform instruction, research indicates that these discussions may not push the PSTs to think critically about what the assessments reveal about students' instructional needs (Gao et al., 2019). Without explicit opportunities to engage in this level of reflection, PSTs may develop assessment practices that are more procedural than purposeful, limiting their ability to use assessment as a tool for enhancing student learning outcomes. Thus, it is vital that PSTs have opportunities to critically consider assessment results and how they can be used to tailor instruction to support student success.

When purposefully utilized, classroom assessment supports differentiated instruction (DI) by providing information about students' current level of skill or knowledge in a specific area. Ongoing assessment that identifies students' level of proficiency in relation to the specific learning targets can also be a tool to support equity within the classroom (Dack et al., 2022). This ongoing assessment also provides opportunities to recognize student growth in skills and knowledge and provides information to guide instruction and plan opportunities for flexible grouping, student reflection, and other strategies to support positive student outcomes.

When planning for implementation of DI, the use of pre-assessments can be utilized to purposefully inform instruction, including information about student misconceptions, background knowledge, and attitudes toward course topics. With that in mind, this chapter will provide sample pre-assessments (assessments of PSTs' prior/existing knowledge or attitudes) and instruction-embedded formative assessments (assessments of PSTs' understanding/retention of information from recent instruction and/or shifts in attitudes) that can be utilized to determine PST background knowledge and needs when introducing new content. Pre-assessments can be utilized to purposefully compact lessons, reducing time and emphasis on concepts or terms that PSTs are already knowledgeable of, allowing opportunities for digging more deeply into content/concepts.

Pre-Assessments

Many of the formative assessments discussed below are well suited for pre-assessment of knowledge and/or attitudes before engaging PSTs with information. These assessments can inform instruction by identifying material that PSTs are already knowledgeable of and can identify PSTs who may need additional support before or during subsequent lessons. In addition, these pre-assessments can be revisited after PSTs have engaged with the material to gauge growth in student knowledge and/or changes in attitudes.

Vocabulary Chart

A vocabulary chart (Table 2) provides the teacher with information regarding students' knowledge and understanding of vocabulary relevant to a specific course or lesson. Although many versions of this chart ask the student to indicate their familiarity with each term by checking a box, I recommend also asking the student to provide their own definition of any term that they indicate they know well enough to do so. This can also help

Table 2 Example Vocabulary Chart

Directions: For each of the following terms, indicate how well you feel that you know/understand the meaning of the term as it is used in education. If you indicate that you can explain it in your own words, do so in the final column.

Term	I have never heard this term.	I have heard this term but do not know what it means.	I know this term but could not explain it.	I know this term and can explain it in my own words.	My definition of this term.
Assessment					
Formative assessment					
Summative assessment					
Diagnostic assessment					
Individualized learning					
Competency-based education					

identify misconceptions students may have about any terms. The results of the vocabulary chart can identify terms that all students are already familiar with that need no further explicit instruction, terms that only a few students need clarified, and terms that should be addressed within whole-class instruction.

Anticipation Guide

An anticipation guide can take a variety of forms. It can include factual statements that students identify as true or false or opinion statements that students can agree or disagree with (Tables 3 and 4). Anticipation guides can also push students' thinking by requiring them to explain their reasoning. They can be used before engaging with information to show students' prior knowledge/attitudes and again after engagement to show growth or change in knowledge/attitudes (Tables 4 and 5). I typically either take these up and make a master sheet of responses to identify trends in responses or (in small classes) make a master sheet as I walk around the room engaging with my PSTs.

Table 3 Example Anticipation Guide (Factual Knowledge)

Directions: Read the following statements, and in the "Before" column, indicate if you feel that each statement is true (T) or false (F). After our lesson, rewrite any false statements to make them true using new information you learned.

Before		After
	Students will learn more effectively if instruction is matched to their preferred learning styles.	
	Spacing out study sessions is an effective strategy for retaining information.	
	Developing your own questions on material is an effective study strategy.	
	Right-brained people are more creative than left-brained people.	
	Cramming before a test is an effective study strategy.	

Answer Key: 1. False; 2. True; 3. True; 4. False; 5. False

Table 4 Example Anticipation Guide B (Factual Knowledge)

Directions: Read the following statements, and in the "Before" column, indicate if you agree or disagree with each statement. After our lesson, indicate if you still agree/disagree with each statement.

Before			After	
Agree	Disagree		Agree	Disagree
		Earthquakes are rare events.		
		Deserts exist in both hot and cold climates.		
		The continents have shifted position as much as they are able.		
		Diamonds are not the only mineral that can cut glass.		
		Volcanoes are found only on land.		
		Toilets flush in opposite directions in the northern and southern hemispheres.		
		A compass always points to true north.		
		The sky is blue because it reflects the blue waters that cover approximately 70 percent of Earth.		

After the unit/lesson, summarize the information that either supported your initial beliefs or caused you to change your mind.

_____

_____

Table 5 Example Anticipation Guide (Attitude)

Directions: Read the following statements and indicate how strongly you agree or disagree with each by marking the appropriate box. Then explain your thinking in one or two sentences.

Statement	Strongly Agree	Agree	Disagree	Strongly Disagree	Explanation
Teachers should utilize a variety of strategies to support students' growth in skills and knowledge.					
Teachers should collaborate with families and communities to support student growth.					
All students within a single classroom should receive identical instruction.					
Students' cultural backgrounds and experiences are important information for teachers to integrate into lesson planning and instruction.					
Students in a single classroom may vary in a variety of ways, including interests, needs, strengths, and levels of motivation.					

After class readings and discussion, review your ratings and explanations. How has your thinking been confirmed or changed?

Journal Prompt

Using a journal prompt pre-assessment provides PSTs with an opportunity to share what they already know about a specific topic. Giving PSTs a limited amount of time for this (such as the one-minute essay; Stanley, 2022) can push them to prioritize the most important information in their brief writing. The completed prompts can then be analyzed by the instructor to identify any misconceptions about the topic as well as areas in which PSTs already have a strong knowledge base. To close out a lesson or unit, PSTs can return to these journal prompts and create an addendum in which they correct and add to their original journal submission. Once I know the needs of the PSTs in my course, I often provide two or three minutes to complete such tasks, as opposed to one, to support those who need more time to process or produce their response.

Example Journal Prompts

- In one minute, explain what you know about teaching mathematical thinking to young children.
- You have two minutes to share what you know about the water cycle.
- In one minute, explain Vygotsky's Zone of Proximal Development.

Entrance Cards

Entrance cards are similar to exit tickets (discussed later in this chapter) but serve as a pre-assessment of student knowledge as opposed to a formative assessment after a lesson. Compared to the journal prompt, an entrance card can provide a more structured prompt to identify prior knowledge as well as any misconceptions. Entrance cards can utilize a variety of prompt types, including asking students to list a certain number of things they know about the topic, identify the steps of a process, or explain a series of steps (Stanley, 2022).

Example Entrance Card Prompts

- What are the Five E's in a 5 E inquiry lesson plan?
- Identify three of the five stages of child development.
- In 10 words or fewer, define summative assessment.

Four Corners

A four-corners activity presents students with a series of multiple-choice questions related to the content they will be engaging with. To prepare, the teacher assigns a letter (A, B, C, D) to each corner of the room (or four different areas if the corners are not accessible). As each question is shared (in my classroom, I project the questions and answer choices on the screen/monitor), students go to the area of the room corresponding with the letter they feel represents the correct answer. The teacher keeps a quick tally chart of how many students chose each answer. The correct answer is then shared with the class. Students who choose the correct answer can then be given an opportunity to share any additional information they know. I have also had students who chose the incorrect answer share why they chose this answer, which helps to identify any misconceptions. (This requires a classroom climate in which students feel comfortable making and learning from mistakes. See Chapter 3 for ideas on creating this environment.) I typically include between five and 10 questions when engaging my students in a four-corners activity. If your classroom space is not conducive to this sort of movement for all your students, this can easily be adapted to utilize a technology tool, such as Kahoot or Plickers, to remove the requirement for movement and allow students to share their responses. (See the end of this chapter for information on technology tools that can be utilized for assessment.)

Example Four-Corners Question Set for a Children's Literature Class Focused on Book Awards (correct answer for each question indicated in bold)

1 The Caldecott Medal is awarded annually to recognize excellence in what aspect of a children's book?
   a. Writing
   b. Illustrating
   c. Sales figures
   d. Diversity

2 Which award is given annually to recognize an exemplary informational book for children?
   a. Newbery Award
   b. National Book Award
   c. Sibert Book Medal
   d. Coretta Scott King Award

3 What is the focus of the Pura Belpré Award?

  a. Books with international themes

  b. Books by Latinx authors and illustrators that celebrate Latino culture and experiences

  c. Books by African American authors and illustrators that explore issues of diversity

  d. Books written in both Spanish and English

4 The Michael L. Printz Award is given annually for excellence in which type of literature?

  a. Young Adult Literature

  b. Middle Grades fiction

  c. Picture Books

  d. Graphic Novels

5 The Schneider Family Book Award recognizes books that best portray:

  a. multicultural experiences and voices

  b. historical events from a critical perspective

  c. scientific information in an accessible format

  d. individuals living with disabilities

Vote with Your Feet

The vote-with-your-feet strategy is typically used to provide students with an opportunity to express their opinion and compare it to their peers. It can also be used like a four-corners activity, but with statements that have binary response possibilities or a series of responses that range from strongly agree to strongly disagree. Students stand in a straight line (one behind the next) with points identified to the right and left to represent the intended responses. As each statement or question is read aloud or shared in writing, students move to the point that identifies their response. As with the four-corners activity, technology tools can be utilized if the classroom space is not conducive to the activity.

Example Vote-with-Your-Feet Activity Script for a Practicum Class Meeting Focused on Identifying Areas for Further Exploration

For the following activity, I need everyone to line up one in front of the other in the center of the room. Make the line as straight as you can. I am going to read a series of statements out loud. For each one, step to the right if you agree with the statement or step to the left if you disagree with the statement. After each statement, we will pause for discussion. The goal of this activity is to identify topics for us to explore in future class meetings.

Statement 1: Reaching out to my students' parents or caregivers is something I find intimidating.

Statement 2: I worry about my ability to handle disruptive behavior in my classroom.

Statement 3: I want to know more about how to balance building positive relationships with my students and maintaining classroom discipline.

Statement 4: I am interested in learning more about strategies for communicating with parents or caregivers.

Statement 5: Balancing my time as a classroom teacher is something I want to learn more about.

Mind Map or Concept Map

Mind maps (also called concept maps; Roberts & Inman, 2015; Stanley, 2022) have been the focus of a number of research studies in various contexts that indicate that this strategy can positively support student outcomes (Hattie, 2024). Compared to the other pre-assessment strategies included within this chapter, mind maps are less rigid and can result in a greater variety of student products. To create the mind map, students first put the topic or central question of the mind map in a circle in the center of a piece of paper (or the center of the screen if a computer program is being used to create the mind map). Students can then create branches from the central hub with categories relevant to the topic, make connections between concepts, and branch out with more specific information where relevant. These subcategories can be assigned by the instructor to provide additional structure or can be left up to the students to determine. Arrows or lines can be utilized to indicate relationships between terms and concepts. Mind maps can also be used to take notes during engagement with content (process differentiation). For example, before a lesson on multitiered systems of

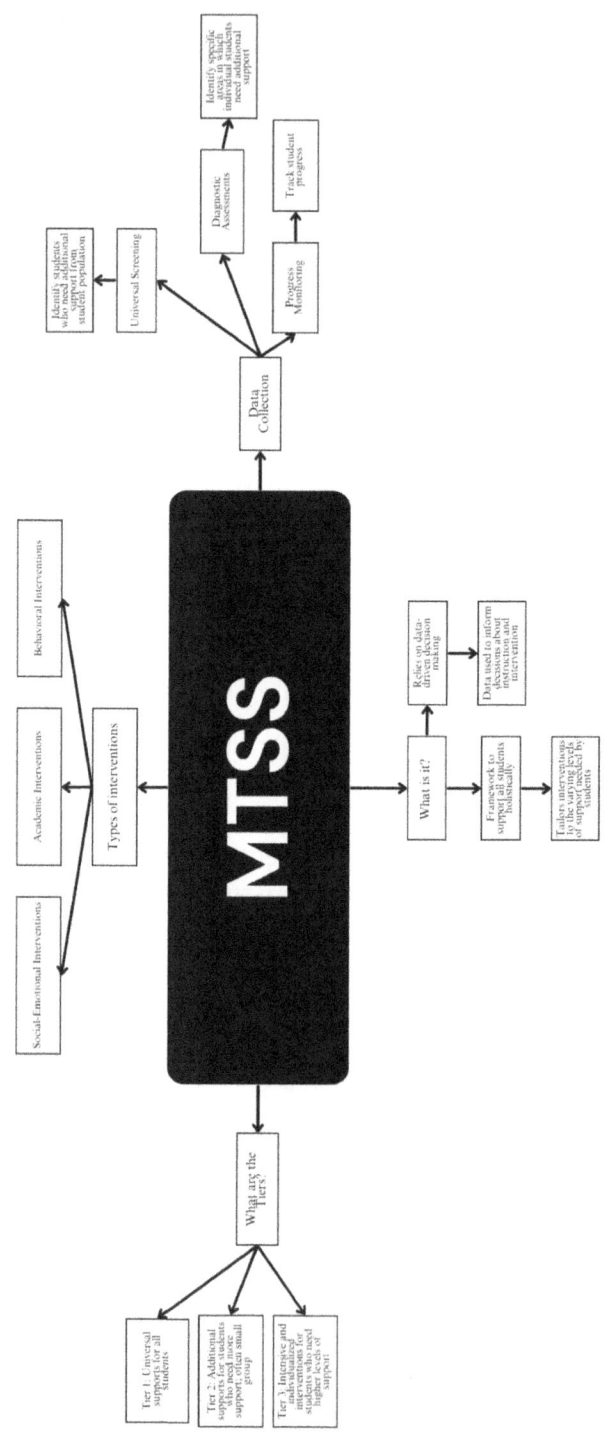

Figure 2 Example Mind Map.

support, PSTs may be given a list of the following subcategories, including definition and purpose, tiers, data collection, and types of interventions, and may also be invited to add any additional categories or subcategories that they feel necessary (Figure 2).

In addition to serving as a pre-assessment, mind maps can also be used as a note-taking tool. As PSTs engage with content, whether through direct instruction or interacting with texts independently or in small groups, they can expand and refine the information in their mind maps. This iterative process encourages deeper comprehension by allowing PSTs to organize information visually, identify patterns and connections, and synthesize new learning. These mind maps then serve as a valuable reference for discussions, collaborative activities, and assessments.

Five Most Difficult Questions

The five-most-difficult-questions pre-assessment (Winebrenner, 1992) allows PSTs who feel confident with their knowledge or skills in a specific area to demonstrate mastery so that they can move ahead or dive more deeply into content. The strategy requires the instructor to identify the five most difficult questions that PSTs should be able to answer at the end of a lesson or unit and allowing those who feel ready to respond to those questions. I have adapted this strategy so that it is both a pre-assessment and a preview of the knowledge or skills that PSTs will gain within the lesson or unit. Thus, all PSTs are asked to consider the five questions, how they might respond to them, and what they expect to learn based on the questions. Those who feel they can already answer the questions are welcome to submit responses, and all PSTs are asked to submit their predictions of what they will be learning based on the five questions.

Instruction-Embedded Assessments

The assessments below can provide in-the-moment feedback for the teacher to utilize in adjusting instruction, determining material that may need to be clarified, or identifying students who need additional support before engaging with more material. Some of these assessments work best at the end of a class session, while others are useful tools for guiding class discussion.

Exit Ticket

At the end of class, students respond to a brief prompt to gauge their understanding of the lesson for the day. These prompts will be similar to the examples given for entrance cards. Students can be heterogeneously grouped for the next class meeting based on understanding of the content with students who "got it" grouped with students who may need additional support. The teacher then provides prompts for small-group discussion focusing on areas where students lacked clarity (Cornelius, 2013). Homogeneous grouping can also be utilized in which the teacher provides additional resources or practice for students who need more engagement with the material covered, while students who show a strong understanding are provided with activities that extend their understanding and require higher levels of synthesis or critical thinking. Which method of grouping to utilize is based on the instructor's knowledge of the students and what will benefit them. I have worked with classes where the PSTs who were confident in the material actively sought opportunities to support their peers through heterogeneous groups and their peers enjoyed this as well and others where PSTs who needed more support were less receptive to learning from their peers and preferred homogeneous groups with more support from me.

3-2-1 Chart

A 3-2-1 chart provides a structure for students to identify main points of what they have learned and to pose remaining questions. The chart can be completed after reading course texts, after a lecture, and so on. Within the chart, students list three new facts or ideas they learned, two facts or ideas they already knew that were confirmed (or two things they found interesting), and one question they still have about the material or topic. When I use this in my courses, I ask each of the students to share their question by writing it up on the whiteboard or sharing it through an electronic tool like Padlet before turning in the completed chart. I spend time answering the students' questions and making note of the questions I cannot immediately answer. I spend some time researching and finding resources for those questions I was not already able to answer and provide these answers and/or resources during the next class meeting so that all questions posed are answered. PSTs in my courses comment on how much they value the additional step of answering their questions, as noted by the following quote:

I'm glad you're taking the time to research and answer our questions. I've never had a teacher do that after a 3-2-1. —Preservice teacher in K–8 ELA methods, spring 2018

In some courses, I have also selected a few questions from the board for PSTs to research in small groups and present their findings to the class. I determine whether to take this step based on the questions that are presented. If there are questions that I know will be difficult to find reliable resources to answer or that may have a lot of misconceptions within the available resources, I make sure to address those myself and to be explicit in addressing the misconceptions. By having PSTs research some of the class's questions, I am also able to support them in identifying and utilizing reputable resources, such as publications and websites of professional and education-focused nonprofit organizations, government organizations, and research journals.

K-W-L Chart

A K-W-L (Know—Want to Know—Learned) chart is a three-column graphic organizer that asks students to respond to two prompts (what you know about the topic and what you want to learn about the topic) before a lesson or unit and complete the final column (what you learned) after the lesson or unit (Ogle, 1986). Studies indicate that K-W-L charts activate students' prior knowledge and assist in student goal setting (Diasti et al., 2023). When I utilize this tool, I make one minor shift that I discovered when I taught middle school. For the W section of the graphic organizer, I shifted the language from "What do you want to know?" (a question to which some middle schoolers responded, "Nothing") to "What do you wonder about this topic?" The first two columns allow me, as the instructor, to identify what the PSTs already know, what misconceptions they may have, and what questions they have that can help shape instruction on the topic. The final column serves as a formative assessment of PST learning. Ideally, their learning will align with their wonderings, but this may not always be the case. In the sample K-W-L chart (Table 6), PSTs are learning about the C3 Framework and how it is utilized in social studies instruction. In this example, PSTs completed the first two columns after a brief reading about the framework but before further instruction. The final column was completed at the end of the lesson.

Table 6 Example Completed K-W-L Chart

Topic: The C3 Framework in Social Studies

What do I know about this topic?	What do I wonder about this topic?	What have I learned about this topic?
The C3 Framework stands for College, Career, and Civic Life.	How does this framework differ from social studies standards?	The C3 Framework is inquiry based and designed to help students develop critical thinking, problem-solving, and participatory skills.
It includes an emphasis on inquiry and real-world application.	What resources are available to help teachers implement the C3 Framework in various grade levels?	The National Council for the Social Studies has resources including publications, webinars, and an annual conference.
It encourages interdisciplinary connections and civic engagement.	How can I assess students' understanding and skills in an inquiry-based model?	Assessment in the C3 Framework can include performance-based tasks, student reflections, and rubrics that measure inquiry skills as opposed to factual recall.
It aligns with social studies disciplines like history, geography, civics, and economics.	How do teachers balance teaching content knowledge with inquiry-based learning?	Effective implementation balances content knowledge by using compelling questions to guide inquiry, ensuring that students engage with key concepts while developing critical thinking.

Muddiest Point

The muddiest point strategy asks students to share what information from the lesson or class session is least clear or most confusing to them (Angelo & Cross, 1993). This provides an avenue for them to identify the areas in which they may need additional support, thus encouraging them to reflect and engage in metacognitive strategies that support their learning. This can be done in a variety of formats, including an exit ticket, a discussion board post (Mackos et al., 2023), or an open-ended survey. Studies investigating the muddiest point strategy in higher education have found it to increase student engagement (Mackos et al., 2023) while also providing information that allows the instructor to tailor future instruction and remediate areas of confusion. While this strategy is often used to allow students to provide anonymous feedback, I strive to create a classroom environment in which PSTs feel comfortable identifying the areas in which they need additional clarity or support. However, there are semesters in which I shift to anonymous submissions if I notice that the responses I am getting from PSTs do not seem to align with their performance on relevant tasks.

Triage Self-Assessment

This self-assessment (Table 7) is an adaptation of the triage chart, a tool used in health care to prioritize care and manage resources. This self-assessment pushes PSTs to reflect on their understanding of the topics, concepts, and vocabulary covered in a lesson or unit and prioritize those in which they are less confident. PSTs can fill out this chart using a list of topics provided by the course instructor, using an outline of the lesson/unit, or brainstorming topics from their notes and other materials. Below is an example of a triage self-assessment after a unit in K–8 mathematics methods focused on teaching fractions.

Table 7 Example Triage Self-Assessment

Unit Topic: Teaching Fractions

Urgent (areas in which I am confused or have a lot of questions I don't know how to find answers to)	Important (areas in which I feel shaky and have a few questions I don't know how to find answers to)	Not Urgent (areas in which I feel confident or feel I have the tools to answer my own questions)
Explaining why fractions with larger denominators (e.g., ¼) are smaller than fractions with smaller denominators (e.g., ⅓).	Using tools like fraction tiles or number lines to explain fraction concepts.	Designing activities that relate fractions to real-world applications (e.g., cooking, measuring).
Teaching how to convert improper fractions to mixed numbers without losing students' understanding.	Helping students compare fractions with unlike denominators using strategies, such as visual aids or cross multiplication.	Using relatable examples, such as dividing food, to introduce fractions.

Note: All assessment ideas listed in this section can be used for ongoing assessment, with some also serving as options for process differentiation (asking different groups of students to complete a different assessment based on their needs, prior knowledge, and so on).

Utilizing Assessment Results to Plan for Instruction

In the following chapters, I will provide a variety of strategies for differentiating instruction through the environment, content, process, and product. However, it is important to provide some clear examples to model how assessment results can be utilized to guide DI. In the examples below, I share how some of the specific pre-assessments discussed in this chapter can be used to help teacher educators plan for differentiation by content, process, and product. Note that within each of these examples, flexible grouping would be utilized. Thus, a PST whose initial pre-assessment shows a need for building foundational knowledge may demonstrate a high level of such knowledge after engaging with content and be prepared for more challenge when the instructor is planning for product differentiation. It is also important to recognize that while all three levels of differentiation will be discussed in the examples below, all three may not be present in every lesson. I have provided examples of content, process, and product differentiation in the three examples below just to demonstrate each level, but including any one of the three levels in any given lesson (and providing PSTs who experience it a chance to reflect on it) will be a valuable experience.

Example 1

Utilizing the vocabulary pre-assessment earlier in this chapter (Table 8) could provide opportunities for differentiation by content and compacting based on PST results. If a small group of PSTs in the course are able to define all terminology in the chart correctly while the remainder of the class has a less concrete grasp of the terms (Table 8), the teacher educator could assign different texts for PSTs to engage with: the first would provide an overview of the assessment and clarify the differences between formative and summative assessment, diagnostic assessment, and so on and would be assigned to the majority of the class based on the pre-assessment results, while the second would push PSTs (such as Ilsa, Eli, and Chris) who are already familiar with and can define the terms to read case studies or research articles that dive deeper into the practical application of different types of assessment or explore more advanced models of assessment, such as portfolios or student self-assessments. This ensures that all PSTs, regardless of their starting point, engage with material that deepens their understanding.

Table 8 Vocabulary Pre-Assessment Results

Term	I have never heard this term.	I have heard this term but do not know what it means.	I know this term but could not explain it.	I know this term and can explain it in my own words.	My definition of this term. (correct)
Assessment	0 PSTs	4 PSTs: Alex, Jordan, Kaisee, Riley	11 PSTs: Avery, Morgan, Dakota, Jamie, Quinn, Syd, Jesse, Robin, Rowan, Charlie, Sky	5 PSTs: Ilsa, Sophie, Noah, Eli, Chris	3 PSTs: Ilsa, Eli, Chris
Formative assessment	2 PSTs: Alex, Jordan	5 PSTs: Kaisee, Riley, Quinn, Jesse, Robin	10 PSTs: Avery, Sophie, Noah, Morgan, Dakota, Jamie, Syd, Rowan, Charlie, Sky	3 PSTs: Ilsa, Eli, Chris	3 PSTs: Ilsa, Eli, Chris
Summative assessment	2 PSTs: Alex, Jordan	5 PSTs: Kaisee, Riley, Quinn, Jesse, Robin	10 PSTs: Avery, Sophie, Noah, Morgan, Dakota, Jamie, Syd, Rowan, Charlie, Sky	3 PSTs: Ilsa, Eli, Chris	3 PSTs: Ilsa, Eli, Chris
Diagnostic assessment	4 PSTs: Alex, Jordan, Quinn, Jesse	8 PSTs: Kaisee, Riley, Morgan, Syd, Robin, Rowan, Charlie, Sky	6 PSTs: Avery, Sophie, Noah, Chris, Dakota, Jamie,	2 PSTs: Ilsa, Eli	2 PSTs: Ilsa, Eli
Individualized learning	4 PSTs: Alex, Jordan, Kaisee, Robin	7 PSTs: Avery, Riley, Dakota, Quinn, Syd, Jesse, Rowan	5 PSTs: Sophie, Morgan, Jamie, Charlie, Sky	4 PSTs: Ilsa, Noah, Eli, Chris	3 PSTs: Ilsa, Eli, Chris
Competency-based education	7 PSTs: Alex, Kaisee, Quinn, Syd, Robin, Rowan, Sky	7 PSTs: Avery, Jordan, Riley, Morgan, Dakota, Jamie, Jesse	1 PST: Charlie,	5 PSTs: Ilsa, Sophie, Noah, Eli, Chris	4 PSTs: Ilsa, Noah, Eli, Chris

In addition to differentiating content, the teacher educator could use the same pre-assessment data, along with an exit ticket addressing what was learned during engagement with content, to differentiate the process by which students engage with the material. For example, PSTs with a solid understanding of the terminology (Ilsa, Eli, and Chris) could work in a small group to analyze the assigned case study or research article and create a visual organizer that illustrates the relationships between different types of assessment and their use within the selected text. Meanwhile, those needing foundational support (those who indicated that they had never heard the majority of the terms) could participate in guided activities, such as instructor-led reading and discussions, that provide additional examples to solidify their understanding of basic terms and concepts. PSTs who demonstrate basic understanding (who indicated that they know most of the terms but could not define them or defined terms in ways that demonstrate some misconceptions) could complete a graphic organizer to define the terms and identify examples within their assigned text(s).

Finally, DI through product differentiation could be utilized, allowing PSTs to demonstrate their understanding at varying levels of complexity. For example, PSTs still needing foundational support after engaging with the information in instructor-guided activities could choose to create a summary or brief presentation describing essential assessment concepts, while those with more advanced knowledge could choose to design a professional development session for their peers, incorporating examples of how to implement various assessment strategies in diverse classroom settings.

Example 2

Using the Anticipation Guide pre-assessment (Table 3), the teacher educator can identify specific misconceptions and varying levels of prior knowledge among PSTs. For example, if a subset of PSTs identifies most statements correctly and provides accurate reasoning, they may have a more advanced understanding of evidence-based learning strategies. In contrast, PSTs with a significant number of misconceptions may need foundational support to better understand cognitive science principles and their application to instruction.

Based on the results of the Anticipation Guide, the teacher educator could provide two sets of resources. For PSTs with a stronger understanding, resources might include research articles and meta-analyses on additional evidence-based practices, such as retrieval practice, interleaving, and spaced repetition. These PSTs could analyze the effectiveness of these strategies in supporting student success and promoting equitable outcomes for diverse learners. For PSTs needing foundational support, resources could include summaries, podcasts, or videos that explain fundamental concepts, such as the lack of evidence to support "learning styles" or how evidence-based practices can be applied to instruction.

For process differentiation, the same resource could be used for all PSTs, with those who already have a strong grasp of concepts engaging independently or in a small group, while PSTs who need more support engage with the text under the guidance of the course instructor. In addition, the teacher educator could use purposeful grouping strategies. PSTs with strong prior knowledge might collaborate in small groups to discuss implementation of proven brain-based instructional strategies in a specific content area or grade-level classroom. Meanwhile, PSTs requiring foundational support could engage in instructor-facilitated activities, such as guided note-taking during a presentation or structured discussions, to clarify misconceptions and reinforce their understanding of the material.

Differentiation could also extend to how PSTs demonstrate their learning (product differentiation). PSTs needing foundational support might create a reflection journal where they rewrite incorrect statements from the Anticipation Guide with evidence-based corrections and include examples of how these concepts could be applied in their future classrooms. PSTs who have already demonstrated foundational understanding could be tasked with creating an infographic or a one-page policy brief with appropriate citations explaining how teachers can integrate evidence-based learning strategies to support equitable outcomes in diverse classroom contexts.

Example 3

Using the prompt "What are the Five E's in a 5 E inquiry lesson plan?" for either an entrance card or exit ticket, the teacher educator can assess PSTs' familiarity with this instructional framework. Responses might range from incorrect or incomplete (e.g., *"Engage, Explore, Establish, Examine"*) to accurate but brief (e.g., *"Engage, Explore, Explain, Elaborate, Evaluate"*) to more detailed answers that include descriptions of each phase. This variety provides insight into PSTs' readiness and areas where additional support may be required.

Based on the responses, the teacher educator could provide differentiated materials (content differentiation). For PSTs struggling to name or define the

5 E's, resources could include an introductory video or infographic outlining each phase of this lesson plan model with examples for practical application. PSTs with a basic understanding could engage with articles or readings exploring how the 5 E model supports inquiry-based learning and addresses diverse student needs. PSTs who demonstrate strong knowledge of the 5 E model could analyze research on the effectiveness of the 5 E model in promoting equitable student outcomes, particularly in underrepresented or marginalized populations.

The learning process could also be adjusted to meet PSTs' needs. Those needing foundational support might participate in a guided activity where they match each phase of the 5 E's with an example from a sample lesson, or they might complete a graphic organizer that defines each phase of the model and compares/contrasts them. PSTs with a moderate understanding could work in pairs to create a basic 5 E lesson plan using a provided template. PSTs with strong knowledge of the framework could collaborate in small groups to design or refine a 5 E lesson plan tailored to meet the needs of a specific student population, such as English learners or students with a specific learning difference.

Differentiation by product would allow PSTs to demonstrate their understanding in varied ways. PSTs needing foundational support might create a visual diagram illustrating the 5 E's with brief descriptions and examples. PSTs with a deeper understanding could write a reflection connecting the 5 E model to other inquiry-based strategies or explaining how they would adapt a phase (e.g., Evaluate) to ensure equity in their future classrooms. PSTs who have demonstrated strong understanding of the 5 E model could design a professional development presentation explaining how the 5 E model fosters inquiry and equity, incorporating data or examples from research.

Goal-Setting Strategies

Another important aspect of assessment in a differentiated classroom is its tie to students' personal goal setting. Students can use pre-assessment results to set learning goals for the lesson or unit and keep track of progress toward these goals through formative assessments and self-assessments. Providing students, including those within TEPs, opportunity to purposefully set the goals and reflect on their progress is an effective strategy for supporting self-efficacy (Moore, 2018), improving academic performance (Morisano et al., 2010; Woelmer et al., 2021), and promoting development of professional identity as an educator. However, much of the research around PST goal setting focuses on clinical placements. Research indicates that when PSTs set goals during their TEP, these goals tend to be focused on classroom management or pedagogical implementation (Moore, 2018). Further, in recent research, each of these two focuses of PST reflection led to different (and positive) outcomes; a focus on classroom management led to an increase in confidence and focus on students, while a focus on pedagogical implementation led to increased feelings of being prepared and creating more efficient lessons (Moore, 2018). Such goal setting provides PSTs with an opportunity to reflect on their own growth and progress. Structured opportunities for setting and reflecting on goals are needed to further support the efficacy of this practice (Travers et al., 2014). Asking PSTs to set short-term learning goals within coursework provides additional opportunities for them to develop their reflection skills and take ownership of their learning throughout their program.

One framework for goal setting is to create SMART goals, an acronym for goals that are specific, measurable, attainable, relevant, and time bound. This is adapted from a framework originally utilized for creating goals in the business world (Doran, 1981) that has since spread to many fields, including education. In my work with students in both K–12 settings and higher education, I have found this framework to be effective for supporting goal setting. However, as with most new (to the students) concepts, modeling and scaffolding are beneficial. To support my PSTs in creating actionable SMART goals, I share an example of my own and discuss how it demonstrates the elements of the SMART goal framework. In a recent semester, I shared this goal with my PSTs: "This semester, I will provide actionable feedback within one week of submission on formative assessments, including one specific strength and one area for growth, to all students who completed the assessment by the due date." In this example, I highlighted the SMART elements within, particularly the elements that make the goal measurable (one strength and one area for growth), since this is an area within the goal structure that I notice many of my PSTs struggle with.

Following that discussion, I provide the following series of prompts to assist PSTs in creating their own SMART goals:

- What is one thing you want to accomplish this semester? (specific)

- How will you know if you are making progress toward your goal? (measurable)
- Is it possible to accomplish this with the time and resources you have? (attainable)
- Are there additional resources you may need to meet your goal? (This question helps me to consider resources that I may need to provide as the course instructor.)
- Why is this goal important to you? (relevant)
- When do you want to meet this goal? (time bound)

Using these prompts, my PSTs write and refine their goal(s) for the semester. Depending on the course, I may ask PSTs to set general goals for the course or specific goals for meeting an identified course learning objective, which often provides me with ideas for additional routes to differentiation through process and product. Finally, I ask PSTs to provide a rationale for their goal(s). Why have they chosen each of the goals they have set? How will meeting this goal impact their success or wellness beyond just the confines of the course? This provides me with additional insight into PSTs' long-term goals and ensure that they are not simply choosing goals to check off a box. Below are some example goals and rationales similar to those that PSTs have set in my courses in previous semesters:

- This semester, I will actively engage in at least two whole-class or small-group discussions per week by sharing questions and ideas or building on peers' contributions and track my participation in a journal to reflect on my growth by the end of the term. This will help me keep myself accountable within this course and build my confidence in speaking up to share ideas and ask questions as I move into student teaching.
- My goal for this semester is to implement an evidence-based classroom management strategy during one of my microteaching demonstrations and reflect on its effectiveness based on peer feedback within two weeks after the demonstration. By working toward this goal, I will also be practicing by using reflection to adjust my instruction.
- This semester, I will visit the university writing center at least three times to improve my academic writing skills, focusing on clarity, structure, and formatting of citations. This goal not only supports my success in this class but also strengthens my overall written communication skills.

- This semester, I will identify and present three teaching strategies aligned with Piaget's stages of cognitive development for abstract concepts, using course resources and additional resources identified in my own reading and research. By using course materials and conducting independent research, I will enhance my ability to critically analyze and apply theoretical knowledge to practical teaching strategies.

Once PSTs have created their goal, I ask them to either highlight or create a chart that identifies each element of the SMART framework. This helps them identify missing components and revise their goals if necessary. Once their goal is set, I ask them to identify actionable steps they can take to meet their goal and write these down as well. These actionable steps can help PSTs see the process to meeting their goal and increase their confidence in their ability to meet it.

Revisiting Goals

Revisiting goals is important for PSTs, as this practice supports critical self-assessment (Miftāḥ et al., 2023) and reflection (Zeichner et al., 2014). The development of reflective practices through revisiting and refining goals can also support the development of PSTs as teacher leaders who have a mindset of continuous improvement (Wang et al., 2022). In addition, providing opportunities to revisit their goals can enhance the confidence of students in higher education, such as PSTs, in their ability to meet these goals (Kimpo & Puder, 2023) and in establishing a growth mindset (Kim et al., 2014; Woods et al., 2024). In both academic and workplace settings, setting and revisiting goals can enhance overall effectiveness (Siech et al., 2022).

Within my courses, I set aside time for PSTs to revisit the goals they set at the beginning of the semester. This can be as little as five minutes to look over their goals and make notes regarding their progress. At the midterm point, I facilitate a discussion with PSTs in my course regarding their progress toward their goals, what resources they may need to meet these goals, and if their goals need to be revised because they were too ambitious, they have already met their initial goal, or their initial goal is no longer relevant. Then I provide time for PSTs to revise their goal if necessary.

Reflection and Discussion Questions

Clark and Rust (2006) posit two guiding questions to use during the process of designing an assessment: "Who will be learning as a result of participating in this assessment process?" and "What will participants be learning?" (p. 74). The reflection questions below will build on these two guiding questions and will also consider the three opportunities for learning from the assessment: while preparing for the assessment, during the assessment, and after assessment results are known and shared (Clark & Rust, 2006).

"As a Teacher Educator" reflection questions are for the course instructor to reflect on their utilization of DI. "As a Learner" and "As an Educator" questions are for PSTs to reflect on their experience with differentiation as a learner and how they can apply that experience to their future classrooms. The two sets of questions consider the dual roles of PSTs in the teacher educator program. It is recommended that PSTs have an opportunity to reflect on these questions individually before sharing and discussing them with peers.

As a teacher educator:

1. Do the assessments in your course provide clear information regarding what students already know or are able to do regarding the learning objective(s) being addressed?
2. Does each assessment come with clear instructions that allow students to focus on showing their knowledge/skill relevant to the learning objective(s) being addressed?
3. Are you providing PSTs with opportunities to experience both formative and summative assessments as students? How do you make these experiences transparent in terms of their pedagogical purpose?
4. Have the PSTs in the course had an opportunity to set learning goals related to the course objectives?
5. How will the process of reflecting on their prior knowledge (e.g., through vocabulary charts or anticipation guides) support PSTs in setting their own learning goals?
6. What actionable steps can you take to differentiate your instruction based on the results of the assessment?
7. How do you encourage PSTs to reflect on the formative assessments you use in class? Do they have opportunities to apply this reflection to their future teaching practice?

8 How will you use the summative assessment results to evaluate the effectiveness of your teaching and the overall learning outcomes for your PSTs?

9 Reflecting on your recent courses, how often do you revisit assessment results to adjust your teaching? How do you communicate these adjustments to your PSTs to model responsiveness in instruction?

As a learner:

1 Do the assessments (formative or summative) in this course have a clear connection to the learning objective(s) for the course?

2 How do you plan to use pre-assessments in this course (e.g., vocabulary charts or anticipation guides) to guide your own learning and identify areas you may need to focus on?

3 Do you have goals for your own learning based on the learning objective(s) for this course?

4 How does the assessment help you see your progress toward your own goals for learning?

5 How can you use self-assessment to gauge your growth in skills and knowledge relevant to the learning objectives for this course?

6 From your perspective, how are assessments used to inform and differentiate instruction in this course?

7 What strategies does your instructor utilize to help PSTs in the course view feedback as a tool for growth and improvement instead of a judgment of their abilities?

As an educator:

1 How will you ensure that your assessments (formative and summative) give you the necessary information you need to guide differentiation in your instruction?

2 How will the insights gained from assessment results (e.g., identifying misconceptions or areas of strength) help you better tailor your instruction to meet diverse student needs?

3 What specific strategies will you use to monitor student growth and development in your classroom? How can you ensure that these assessments are meaningful for students?

4   How can you incorporate self-assessment practices in your future classroom to encourage students to reflect on their own learning?
5   In what ways will you guide students in setting their own learning goals based on self-assessment and feedback from others?
6   How will you foster an environment that encourages growth and learning, even for students who are less successful with traditional assessments?
7   What strategies will you use to help students view feedback as a tool for improvement rather than as a judgment of their abilities?
8   Reflect on your experiences and those of your peers with DI as a learner. How can you adapt the strategies that you and your peers have experienced to address the diverse cultural and academic backgrounds of students in your future classroom?

Additional Technology Tools for Assessment

Kahoot: www.kahoot.com

Kahoot basic is free and allows up to 40 players per game with multiple-choice questions. Players can play solo or in teams with up to five teams with the free account. Students or teams earn points based on how quickly they select the correct answer. Kahoot can also be assigned for students to do outside of class.

Plickers: www.plickers.com

Plickers free edition requires some setup by the instructor to use. Plickers utilizes printed cards with QR codes that are scanned by the teacher to collect students' responses to multiple-choice questions. Students are assigned a card number, which allows the teacher to tie responses to specific students. With the free account, the teacher can set up unlimited classes and create questions sets with an unlimited number of questions. One nice feature of Plickers is the ability to add questions on the fly.

Blooket: www.blooket.com

Blooket is similar to Kahoot but has multiple game modes. With a free starter account, 60 players can be engaged with a single question set. The free account opens more than 10 different game modes. Blooket can also be assigned for students to do outside of class.

Mentimeter: https://www.mentimeter.com

Mentimeter is an online tool that allows educators to engage students in real time using polls, quizzes, and other interactive questions formats. Students respond using their computers or phones. The free account allows for 50 participants per month.

Canva: www.canva.com

Canva has a variety of templates available for brainstorming, including a mind-mapping template. The free account provides access to a variety of templates that can be utilized for instruction. The limit on free accounts is currently 5 GB of cloud storage.

Miro: www.miro.com

Miro is an online mind-mapping tool and offers a free version limited to three editable boards/maps. Miro allows for collaborative mind mapping, allowing multiple individuals to engage with a single map on different devices at the same time.

3 Differentiation by Environment

One thing that I really liked about today's session, was that you give everyone a chance to speak. You also make great connections with your students when they share their thoughts, which makes the environment more inviting and, at least for me, makes me feel more willing to share my thoughts and ideas.
—Preservice teacher in K–8 language arts methods course, fall 2020

When I discuss differentiating by environment, my conceptualization of this aspect of differentiation involves two elements: (1) creating a welcoming classroom environment in which differentiated instruction (DI) can be utilized effectively by setting expectations for preservice teachers (PSTs) to be able to engage with content in multiple ways and (2) creating a physical environment that provide PSTs with opportunities to work in an environment that is both comfortable and productive for them through various strategies, such as grouping formats, seating arrangements, and engagement approaches. Let's look at each of these components on its own to further identify elements of classroom environment that contribute to effective DI by environment.

Creating a Welcoming Classroom Environment

The first element focuses on establishing a classroom environment in which students feel a sense of belonging and a level of safety that encourages intellectual risk-taking. A common phrase heard lately is "Maslow before Bloom's," pointing out the importance of an individual's basic needs being met before they can truly engage in the learning process. This aligns with the care theory of Noddings (2019), in which the needs of students and the building of relationships are considered by the instructor as essential elements of the classroom. As an instructor within the teacher education program (TEP), this includes setting up a classroom environment in which PSTs feel comfortable taking risks and being challenged. In addition, it is important for me, as an instructor, to know the resources available to students and connect my PSTs with those resources to support their success and well-being when appropriate. This includes academic supports, such as the writing center; basic needs supports, such as the campus food pantry; and mental wellness supports, such as the university's counseling and psychological services. As a first-generation college student, I was unaware of all the services available through the college I attended, so I am mindful that PSTs in my classes may need guidance to find resources that will support their success and well-being.

High Expectations and Success for All

Within the first couple of class meetings, I work to share my expectations for the class with the students. Although the bulk of these expectations are laid out in the syllabus, having the opportunity to discuss what these expectations look like in practice supports the PSTs in my classroom in successfully meeting them. For example, many syllabi have statements regarding grading and late-work policies. As I discuss my late-work policy with the class, I share that I plan my calendar around due dates just as they do. If a project is due on a Sunday night by midnight, I have set aside time in my calendar to grade that project in the following days to ensure that everyone gets timely, actionable feedback. Students have commented that this clarification helps them see the need to meet these due dates as less arbitrary and more directly in their best interests. I also encourage PSTs to reach out to me ahead of time if they anticipate or identify challenges to complete an assignment so that we can discuss possible solutions.

Speaking of due dates, there is one strategy I use that the PSTs in my courses truly appreciate: I work with each class to collaboratively set due dates for major assignments in the class. During the second week of class, I ask all students to bring in the announced due dates for major assignments in all their other courses. As they come to class that day, I ask them to add their due dates on the whiteboard or in a shared online document (depending on the classroom layout or the class modality). If someone has already put up an assignment that another PST also must complete, they put a tally mark next to the assignment to show how many are affected by that particular assignment. Once all these established due dates have been shared, I outline the major assignments for my course and discuss each assignment briefly, including how some assignments build on each other. Then we collaborate to come up with due dates for my class assignments. As we determine each due date and PSTs add it to their calendar, I also add grading time for each assignment to my calendar. Since I began implementing this process, I have seen fewer late assignment submissions and a better quality of work since PSTs aren't rushing to do my assignments in the same week another course's major assignment is due. I have worked in TEPs where all instructors met at the beginning of the semester and collaborated on due dates across courses to ensure that PSTs are not overwhelmed with assignments in short bursts with periods of nothing in between. This was also effective, particularly when the instructors were transparent about this process with the PSTs.

I share with my classes my belief that everyone can succeed in the class, and then we discuss specific strategies for supporting success, including time management and planning, reaching out to me early if they need assistance or have a question, and using on-campus supports, such as the writing center and peer tutoring. To reinforce these strategies, I provide concrete examples of when to use them and how they can contribute to their success. I also have students set a goal for the semester (see information on goal setting in Chapter 2) and, in classes where it is possible, meet with each student for a moment to discuss their goal, what resources they will utilize to work toward their goal, and how I can help support them in meeting their goal.

I have been fortunate to attend multiple professional development opportunities focused on proficiency-based education, and these have influenced some elements of my practice that support student self-efficacy and growth within my courses. Among these are providing opportunities for PSTs to revise or resubmit work that doesn't demonstrate proficiency with additional support provided. For example, PSTs who need additional support in writing clearly and coherently (one of the professional proficiencies of our TEP program) based on a submitted task are guided to the university's writing center and are allowed to resubmit the task along with evidence they utilized the services of the writing center. In another example, PSTs whose understanding of pedagogy is not yet evidenced in a task may be provided additional instruction and resources to clarify misconceptions, after which they are given an opportunity to revise and resubmit the assessment with citations for the additional resources included in their revision. While this does mean some additional work for me in grading these revisions, it also allows me to model elements of proficiency-based education, which is being adopted in schools across my state (Montana) and the nation (Stanford, 2023), within my courses.

Supporting Risk-Taking

Supporting PSTs' comfort in taking risks and actively engaging in class are also important aspects of creating a classroom environment in which they feel welcomed and safe. This can be supported in a variety of ways, but two of the most effective in my experience are by modeling risk-taking myself and being honest and open when I need to make changes to improve my instruction. I also acknowledge when I don't know the answer to a student question or when an activity doesn't work as planned. In both cases, I troubleshoot in the moment and share how I can continue to improve or grow my knowledge and instruction. By serving as a model for both taking risks and being open to continued growth in my teaching practice, I am creating an environment in which PSTs can feel confident in stretching themselves and learning from mistakes.

I also strive to create a learning environment where PSTs feel safe to take academic risks by emphasizing growth and improvement rather than perfection. In addition to providing timely feedback, I ensure that my comments are specific, actionable, and framed in a way that encourages reflection and revision. This approach helps PSTs view feedback as a tool for learning rather than as a judgment of their abilities. For example, when providing feedback on a written product that doesn't show clear understanding of concepts learned in class, my feedback might read "Consider how to explain formative and summative assessment to someone who has no background in education. Writing for an audience who needs to build background will help you to explain both terms more clearly" instead of "Definitions not clear. Please rewrite." By focusing on guiding questions and constructive suggestions, I reinforce the idea that learning is an ongoing process, allowing PSTs to develop confidence in refining their work and experimenting with new ideas.

Another strategy for supporting PSTs' engagement and willingness to take risks is the use of collaborative, low-stakes activities. Such activities provide opportunities for PSTs to utilize their strengths and to lean on the strengths of peers while also sharing the risk across group members. This strategy not only fosters a sense of shared responsibility but also encourages deeper engagement with the material, as students feel more comfortable exploring challenging concepts in a risk-reduced setting.

In my courses, this strategy has proven particularly effective for tasks that require higher-order thinking and the application of complex ideas. For example, when tackling case studies for the first time, PSTs may initially feel uncertain about how to critically analyze real-world scenarios. However, by working in teams, they can discuss different perspectives, challenge each other's assumptions, and collectively develop well-reasoned analyses. Similarly, when asked to synthesize course material into a visual representation such as a concept map or infographic, PSTs can collaborate to organize their thoughts, identify key themes, and express their understanding creatively. These experiences not only help PSTs develop essential critical thinking and communication skills but also instill confidence in their ability to engage with course materials and concepts in meaningful ways.

Supporting Autonomy

For PSTs to actively engage in the classroom and take ownership of their learning, they need meaningful opportunities for autonomy. When PSTs have a voice in their educational experience, they develop a sense of agency, become more invested in their work, and strengthen critical decision-making skills that will serve them in their future classrooms. Providing structured choices not only empowers PSTs but also encourages them to think metacognitively about their own learning processes and goals. By intentionally scaffolding these choices, educators can support PSTs in developing confidence, self-regulation, and the ability to make informed instructional decisions.

In my courses, I integrate opportunities for PSTs to make decisions about their learning experience in ways that promote both accountability and engagement. For example, allowing PSTs to collaborate on setting due dates fosters a sense of shared responsibility while also helping them develop time management skills. Engaging in peer feedback allows PSTs to take on an evaluative role, refining their ability to give and receive constructive input—an essential skill for both teaching and lifelong learning. Additionally, offering choices in how they demonstrate their learning, such as through choice boards or alternative project formats (Chapter 6), enables PSTs to showcase their understanding in ways that align with their strengths and interests. These strategies not only enhance motivation but also prepare PSTs to create similarly student-centered learning environments in their future classrooms, reinforcing the value of autonomy in fostering deep, meaningful learning.

Co-constructing assignment rubrics, in particular, not only supports student autonomy but may also support student self-regulation (Fraile et al., 2017) and task performance (Becker, 2016; Fraile et al., 2017). When students participate in defining assessment criteria, they gain a clearer understanding of expectations, which can improve their ability to plan, monitor, and evaluate their own work. While this collaboration takes time within the classroom, I have found it to be time well spent due to increased student buy-in and more positive instructor–student relationships. In addition, engaging in these collaborative processes also helps PSTs develop professional skills they will later apply in their own classrooms, such as designing fair and transparent assessment tools and fostering a classroom culture of shared responsibility in learning.

Another strategy for supporting student autonomy is providing rationales for the topics and activities in class so that PSTs see the relevance of these to their development as educators and to their future classroom practice (Patall & Zambrano, 2019). So, when I ask my PSTs to create a tutorial to introduce an evidence-based teaching strategy to classroom teachers, I include the following rationale: "The goal of this assignment is to provide you an opportunity to explore a specific evidence-based teaching strategy or activity and then explain how to effectively utilize it in your own words. This is preparation for being not just a teacher but a professional colleague who can share knowledge." By framing the assignment in this way, I emphasize that their learning extends beyond their own practice; they are developing the ability to communicate effectively with fellow educators, contribute to a professional learning community (PLC), and advocate for instructional strategies that improve student outcomes. This rationale helps PSTs recognize that their role as educators goes beyond the classroom and includes collaboration, leadership, and lifelong learning, reinforcing the importance of autonomy and self-directed professional development.

Creating a supportive classroom environment in which all students see themselves as part of a community of learners is a vital step in successfully implementing DI within the classroom. When students feel valued, respected, and connected, they are more likely to engage in learning, take academic risks, and collaborate meaningfully with their peers. This emphasis on a positive and inclusive classroom environment also aligns with culturally responsive teaching (CRT), which connects the need for creating a safe space within the classroom where students feel comfortable taking risks, making mistakes, and engaging in respectful disagreements with their peers (Kieran & Anderson, 2019) while also supporting positive identity development and promoting student voice (Morton & Dyer, 2022). On the teacher's part, CRT also requires a shift away from deficit-based thinking within the classroom and more of a critical analysis of the historical and societal why behind this thinking (Morton & Dyer, 2022). Indeed, scholars have provided explicit connections between implementation of CRT and DI within the classroom in areas such as literacy learning (Morton & Dyer, 2022). Within teacher education, fostering an inclusive and caring classroom environment is of particular importance, as studies indicate that one of the top skills PSTs hope to develop during their teacher preparation programs is the ability to create a respectful and supportive space for their future students (Clark & Byrnes, 2015). By integrating CRT and DI principles into their practice, PSTs not only learn to implement effective instructional strategies but also gain the tools to build classrooms that are equitable, responsive, and conducive to meaningful learning for all students.

Strategies for Differentiation by Environment

The Physical Environment

Unlike the pre-K–12 world in which PSTs will be working, many teacher educators have limited opportunities for setting up the physical environment of their classroom. Spaces are often "theirs" only for the period in which their class meets, and any furniture that has been shifted needs to be returned to its original position before the next class (and instructor) enters the space. Despite this limitation, there are things that can be done to make the space "yours" (for both you and your students).

If you are fortunate, the furniture in the room is easily shifted from one configuration to another, providing opportunities for individual and small-group work. When I am in such a classroom, I typically have two or three configurations that I utilize: one that is the typical setup for that classroom (always identified as setup 1 since it is how the classroom should look when we leave) and at least one that shifts students into a pattern that is conducive to small-group discussions if setup 1 does not do so already. I take photos of the classroom in each configuration and put them up on-screen if the PSTs in the class need a reminder of how the classroom should look in each setup. In some classrooms, there is already a visual showing how the room should look when the next class enters, and this becomes setup 1.

I often have PSTs in my classes create visuals or similar tools on chart paper that we may use more than once. When these are on paper with a sticky strip at the top, I have students take them down at the end of class, and we put them back on the pad of paper they came from so I can bring them back in the next class. If they are not on sticky paper, I have used clothes hangers made for pants (the kind that have clips on the hanger) to collect and keep the papers together and safely stored between classes. In some cases, if the classroom is used by the same set of instructors regularly, there can be opportunities to share the space and leave these tools up between classes. For example, I was in a classroom for multiple semesters that was consistently used by three other instructors. We met and divided up the wall space in the classroom so that each of us had an "anchor space" for posting things that needed to be up all semester while also leaving an area that was always cleared between classes for things that needed to be up only during a single class session. This turned out to be beneficial to the instructors and the PSTs in our courses, as both groups were able to reference materials in the room from the other courses to make interdisciplinary and cross-course connections and use a common language thanks to these visual reminders.

Providing Quiet Spaces and Collaborative Spaces

During differentiated activities, there may be a variety of tasks occurring within the classroom at the same time, including opportunities for collaborative and individual work. However, trying to read an article or listen to a podcast while a group of peers is engaging in discussion of a case study in the same classroom space can be difficult for students who need fewer distractions in order to focus. To prevent frustration and support success for all PSTs in my course, I identify a quiet area near my classroom that PSTs can go to when working independently. This may be a small alcove down the hall or a common area that has little traffic during class times. When PSTs choose to use these spaces, we agree on the location they can be found and the time they need to return to class. I ask them to set an alarm on their watch or phone to remind them when it is time to return. On days when we are having multiple small-group discussions all at once, I typically try to find additional spaces for groups to meet so that members in each group can focus effectively.

Welcoming PSTs at the Door

Welcoming each individual as they enter the classroom is a powerful way to build positive relationships with PSTs in your courses and support their sense of belonging in your class, even if the instructor does not know each student by name (Sandstrom, 2023). Greeting PSTs at the door of the classroom, including making eye contact, may communicate to them the instructor's genuine desire to connect with and support them. Beyond a quick hello, the instructor can connect with PSTs based on their knowledge of the students' lives outside class by asking questions about the activities they engage in and other interests outside the classroom.

Welcoming PSTs at the door also provides the instructor with a quick way to gauge PSTs' mood and well-being as they enter class and invites PSTs to pause and share ideas or concerns. Because I am accessible during this initial entry time in class, PSTs who are dealing with personal or academic challenges often use this time to touch base or to set up a time for us to meet to discuss their concerns. I have also used this time to reengage PSTs who have missed class meetings.

The Virtual Environment

In programs that are hybrid or fully online, it is important to consider how the virtual classroom space's organization can support PST engagement and help create an environment in which they feel safe taking risks and have opportunities to engage with their peers.

Clear expectations and organization: I often hear my PSTs comment that each of their instructors sets up their course differently in the university's learning management system. While it would be ideal for there to be consistency in course setup, in the absence of this consistency, there are things we can do to support PSTs in navigating the virtual environment of our courses. This can be as simple as including a to-do list or checklist with due dates at the beginning of each module and can include additional tools, such as an introductory video for each module in which the instructor walks through the assigned readings and tasks. Students in my fully online courses appreciate this structure, as indicated by the following comment:

> I have appreciated the thought and variety [Dr. Pennington] puts into her weekly lessons and activities and that she regularly takes the time to record a video to go through the week's materials. Those videos and her weekly checklist really made clear what was expected from us. —Preservice teacher in secondary teaching methods (semester course evaluation), fall 2024

Encourage Peer-to-Peer Interaction

Fostering meaningful peer-to-peer interaction is crucial for students to feel connected and supported in a virtual environment. To facilitate this, consider breaking up the class into smaller, rotating groups for collaborative work. For example, assign students to groups for weekly discussion boards, group projects, or virtual study sessions. By rotating groups throughout the semester, students are encouraged to interact with a wide variety of peers, providing opportunities to engage with peers with different backgrounds and perspectives.

Additionally, establish peer mentoring or peer feedback opportunities. In structured peer review assignments, students can give and receive feedback on assignments or presentations. To ensure that the feedback remains constructive and helpful, consider providing feedback guidelines or rubrics so that students know how to provide feedback that supports the growth of their peers.

Interactive group activities, such as brainstorming sessions, collaborative whiteboards, and virtual role-playing, allow students to take risks in a less formal context. These group activities provide a low-pressure environment for students to express ideas, solve problems, and get immediate responses from peers.

One common strategy is the use of breakout rooms in videoconferencing tools. The instructor can assign small groups to work on a discussion question or problem for a set time, then have them share their insights with the larger group. This strategy allows PSTs to collaboratively tackle questions or prompts that require critical thinking before addressing a larger audience.

Discussion Boards

Discussion boards are an often-utilized tool in online learning environments. One of the concerns regarding these is the potential for students to pull pieces of peers' responses instead of creating their own original post. This can be addressed by changing the setting of the discussion board so that students cannot see the posts of their peers until they have posted to the board, which also addresses students' concerns that they will post something that has already been posted. Another approach that I have taken when engaging my online students in discussion boards is to have PSTs post their initial contribution one week and respond to peers the following week. This allows everyone the time they need to thoughtfully craft their posts (both initial post and peer responses) more effectively than I saw when my PSTs were expected to complete all posts (initial and responses to peers) in a single week.

Setting Clear Expectations and Norms

Establishing clear expectations and norms is foundational for creating a safe and respectful virtual environment. At the start of the course, explicitly outline behavioral expectations, such as guidelines for respectful communication, active participation, and timely responses. Consider cocreating some of these norms with your students by engaging them in a discussion or survey about what they feel would create a safe space for everyone. This not only helps PSTs feel heard but also encourages a shared responsibility for maintaining a positive online environment.

For example, the instructor could post a "Community Guidelines" document at the beginning of the course that covers expectations for tone, language, and how students should engage with one another, especially in difficult or contentious topics. Incorporate structured guidelines for peer feedback, including using phrases such as "I appreciate your perspective because…" or "What I learned from your post is…" to promote constructive dialogue. Reinforce these expectations by returning to them regularly, especially when addressing any concerns, and by offering specific praise when PSTs uphold these norms.

It is also important to create a safe space for disagreements. Encourage students to challenge ideas respectfully, especially when the content is complex or controversial. You can emphasize that different perspectives are not only valid but also necessary for deeper learning. By modeling active listening and acknowledging students' contributions, you reinforce the idea that every student's voice is valuable.

Regular Check-Ins

Set up regular individual or group check-ins to gauge PST comfort levels, challenges, and progress. When students feel that their concerns are being heard and addressed, they are more likely to take academic risks and engage with their peers. Consistent and intentional check-ins are vital to gauge students' well-being, academic progress, and comfort level within the virtual classroom. One way to facilitate this is by incorporating weekly or biweekly individual check-ins, which can be as simple as a brief survey or a check-in e-mail asking about their understanding of the course content, any difficulties they're facing, or any emotional challenges they may be experiencing. For example, a short survey could include questions such as "What part of the course material do you find most challenging?" or "Do you feel supported in this course? If not, how can I assist?"

Additionally, consider using anonymous feedback tools like course polls to allow students to voice concerns without fear of being singled out. Anonymous check-ins help students feel safe sharing issues they may be too uncomfortable to raise publicly. After reviewing this feedback, make sure to respond promptly by adjusting the course materials, offering additional resources, or providing clarification in class. By responding to students' concerns, you demonstrate that their input matters and that the class is an adaptive and responsive space. (Read more on specific approaches for inviting student feedback later in this chapter.)

In terms of group dynamics, implementing "pulse checks"—quick assessments of students' feelings about the class environment—can be particularly useful. Ask simple questions, such as "How comfortable do you feel asking questions in the class?" or "Do you feel you have the resources you need to succeed?" These pulse checks give you a snapshot of the collective mood and learning environment. After receiving the results, offer targeted support or small adjustments to improve the environment and better meet students' needs.

Moreover, TEP faculty can incorporate "virtual office hours" or drop-in sessions where students can have one-on-one discussions with the instructor, especially if they want to address concerns or seek additional guidance in a less formal context. The availability of this time helps build stronger connections with PSTs and provides a reliable channel for continuous support.

Think Time

Utilizing think time is a strategy that took me time to use effectively as a teacher. When I first attempted it, I simply wasn't waiting long enough; the silence made me uncomfortable! This is a common observation when I am supervising PSTs in their field experiences as well—giving the students in their class quiet time to consider their response leaves the PSTs feeling awkward in the quiet. I pushed past this by directly stating how long think time would be (15 seconds? 30 seconds?) and then watching the minute hand on the clock or setting a timer to make me accountable for providing that time. I share the expectation with those in my course that no one should raise their hand to respond until think time is over. Since all PSTs in the class have had an opportunity to consider their response, I am able to hear from a variety of individuals in my classes. I have had PSTs comment that the think time encourages them to engage more actively since they know I won't just call on the first person to raise their hand and then move on to the next question or prompt.

Strategies to Set the Stage

Pronouncing Names Correctly

In an increasingly diverse world, teachers and teacher educators will come across names from a variety of cultures as well as names that use nontraditional spellings. When educators take the time to learn and correctly pronounce students' names, they communicate respect and recognition, reinforcing students' sense of identity and belonging within the learning space. Mispronouncing a student's name, even unintentionally, can lead to feelings of exclusion or discomfort, whereas making the effort to say it correctly fosters trust and positive student–teacher relationships. This seemingly small yet significant effort can contribute to a more welcoming classroom climate where all students feel seen and valued for who they are. Proper pronunciation of students' names is not only a meaningful step toward showing students they are valued within the classroom; it can also support motivation within courses (Murdoch et al., 2018). Recent research indicates that about half of international college students saw proper pronunciation of their names to be important and can support positive adjustment and feelings of belonging (Zhang & Noels, 2021). Beyond the initial introduction, consistently using students' names correctly throughout the semester further reinforces their sense of inclusion and respect. As students introduce themselves, I take notes of name pronunciation on my attendance sheet, repeat their name to make sure I am pronouncing it correctly, and ask for clarification if needed. Additionally, I make a conscious effort to model this practice for students, encouraging them to learn and correctly pronounce each other's names as part of building an inclusive and respectful classroom community.

Knowing Your PSTs

One of the most effective ways to create a welcoming environment within the classroom is to be purposeful in knowing the PSTs in your courses. This includes knowing their names and their interests. This can be supported by introductory activities (see below) or student surveys.

Introductory Peer Interviews

Instead of asking PSTs to introduce themselves, I sometimes ask them to find a peer they don't already know well and interview that person so they can introduce them to the class. These one-on-one conversations with a peer provide time for small-scale community building and lead to much more interesting introductions than if PSTs introduced themselves due to the follow-up questions and conversation that are part of the interview. Questions can start with the basics (name, year in college, hometown, etc.) and then get much more creative (surprising fact about yourself, favorite teacher ever, describe your dream school). I typically have no more than four or five questions for the sake of time. As each person is introduced, I ask them to either stand or wave to the class so that everyone can see who is being introduced.

Stand Up/Hand Up

Finding connections among the members of the classroom community is an important step to building a positive environment in which all feel a sense of belonging. One strategy I have used to help build this sense of belonging from day one is the stand-up/hand-up activity. As PSTs introduce themselves, others who have a similar response either stand up or put their hand up (depending on the space and needs of the PSTs in the course). For example, a question I often have PSTs respond to when introducing themselves in my English language arts methods class is to share one memory they have of elementary reading class. Many share the experience of reading to earn points through a computer program. As this is shared by one individual, many others stand up to indicate that this is a strong memory for them as well. As folks stand up (or put their hands up), there is a moment of recognition and sharing between those standing and the person who originally shared. Once an idea or memory is shared, PSTs are welcome to choose another to share when their turn comes.

Name Tents

I will confess to not always being the fastest at remembering names. In large classes, I often ask PSTs to create name tents on the first day of class and to continue using them for the first few class meetings. On their name tents, I ask them to include their name and visuals (words or pictures) to respond to other prompts that help me and their peers get to know them. I give them a few minutes to create their name tent, then we use the name tents as talking points for class introductions. Prompts, in addition to their name, will vary based on the course but could include anything from "How I feel about (topic, i.e., math, science, etc.)" to "My ideal classroom."

Memories on a Mug

One semester in particular, I had an 8:00 a.m. class that was very content heavy. This wasn't my first time teaching an early morning class (with the first class meeting of the semester on a Monday, no less!), and I was aware that many of the PSTs in my class might not be as engaged as I would like due to the early morning time slot and may be, in fact, suffering from a lack of sleep due to the early class time (Yeo et al., 2023). I wanted to set a positive and welcoming tone from the first day of class but was unsure of how to combat the early morning effects. I stopped by the classroom space and noticed that there was a sink in the room. And an idea was born. On the first day of class, each PST was given a plain white mug and some paint markers to use to decorate it. These were decorated similarly to a name tent and were used to provide talking points for introductions. These remained on a rolling cart that I brought to each class meeting, along with an electric kettle and a tub of hot chocolate mix. PSTs were welcome to grab a hot drink at any time before or during class. Many brought teas and coffee to share. A small coffeepot was added to the cart by a PST in the second week of the course. At the end of the semester, each PST took their mug home as a memento of the course and the learning community we had built.

Student Questionnaires

One tool that I have seen many of my peers utilize to get to know the PSTs in their classes is a quick questionnaire completed during the initial class meeting. This can be done electronically or on paper. Prompts can include student demographic information (e.g., major, standing [sophomore/junior/senior], past coursework in the content area) and questions to help the instructor learn more about each student's background and interests. Such questionnaires should be short, so focus on the information that will be most useful to you as the instructor. For example, if all PSTs in a course have a required set of prerequisites for the course, it may be less useful to ask about previous coursework.

Example Student Questionnaire

Welcome to (class name)! This survey is to help your instructor get to know you and to help your instructor consider how to best support you this semester. Please answer all questions you are comfortable responding to. All information collected will be kept confidential and will be accessed only by the instructor and teaching assistant.

Name: _____
What do you prefer to be called? _____
Preferred e-mail address: _____
College Standing (circle one): Freshman Sophomore Junior Senior Other: _____
Major: _____

1. Why are you taking this course?
2. What do you want to gain from this course?
3. What do you already know about (course topic)?
4. What other responsibilities do you have outside this course that your instructor should be aware of?
5. What would you like your instructor to know about you?

Additional prompts for student questionnaires

- What interests you about this course?
- What other coursework have you taken in (course topic)?
- What kinds of support will be most helpful for you to support your success in this course?
- When was the last time you took a class on (course topic)? Was it a positive experience? Explain.
- What should your instructor avoid doing in class in order to support your success?
- What challenges or concerns do you anticipate facing in this course, and how do you think you can overcome them?
- What would a successful semester look like to you, and how can we work together to achieve that?

Grouping Strategies to Encourage Student Interaction

Flexible grouping strategies are a key component of DI, allowing students to engage in varied collaborative learning experiences based on their needs and strengths. These strategies include homogeneous grouping, where students work with peers who share similar skill levels or learning needs, as well as heterogeneous grouping, which encourages collaboration among students with diverse abilities and perspectives (Gheyssens et al., 2020). By incorporating both types of grouping, instructors can target specific learning objectives while also fostering peer learning and engagement.

In TEPs, flexible grouping can be intentionally integrated into coursework to mirror practices that PSTs may later use in their own classrooms. PSTs quickly recognize that they will not be working with the same small group throughout the semester; instead, they will be strategically grouped and regrouped based on the goals of a given activity. For example, in one session, PSTs may be grouped by content familiarity, allowing those with prior knowledge of a topic to engage in extension tasks, while those newer to the concept receive scaffolded support. In another session, heterogeneous groups may be used to encourage peer teaching and collaborative problem-solving. By experiencing firsthand the benefits of flexible grouping, PSTs gain confidence and competence in applying similar strategies with their own students.

Clock Buddies

One tool that I used to encourage students to engage with a variety of discussion partners across the semester was "Clock Buddies." This strategy requires a little preparation in the form of handouts of a clock with a blank by each hour or by having students draw this format while showing an example on the screen. Students then mix and mingle to fill their clock. If student A puts student B in the 1:00 slot, then student B should do likewise and put student A in the 1:00 slot. In small classes, I use only even-numbered hours, so students have six different buddies, while larger classes use the full 12 hours, resulting in 12 different buddies. When I want students to pair up, I indicate which hour buddy they should meet with: "For this next activity, please work with your 10:00 buddy." If the buddy listed for that hour is absent, the students are instructed to shift to the next hour and join that buddy and their partner. In content classes, I sometimes get creative and name the hours differently, such as naming each hour after an author for a children's literature class or after a type of statistical analysis in a quantitative research class.

Preassigned Groups

After an assessment, I look over the student scores and identify students who may need additional support or clarification on any concepts assessed. I use this information to create small groups for the next class session. Thus, if there are concepts that a small number of students need clarification on, I group those students together. As students enter, I ask them to sit at the table listed on the screen. I share the results of the assessment as well as the trends I noticed. I follow up with discussion and reflection questions for students to discuss with their groups, along with a product of some sort to create based on the discussion (see Chapter 6 for ideas and examples). As groups are meeting, I rotate from group to group to reteach or clarify the concept needed by each group or to provide opportunities for additional exploration and application for groups who have shown mastery of the current skills or content. If I want to provide a variety of activities for PSTs in my courses to engage in to either strengthen or extend their skills and knowledge (as needed), I may also use a task chart (Chapter 4) with preassigned groups. Groups formed for this purpose are typically fluid in that grouping will shift based on the results of the next assessment opportunity.

Another way I create preassigned groups is by asking students to rate topics in order of their interest in learning more about that specific topic. For example, in my ELA methods course, students work in PLCs to take a deep dive into a specific literacy topic or student subpopulation of interest. I list the potential topics on the board and ask students to order their top three choices from those listed. I then use this information to create the PLCs. Often, there is a lot of interest in one or two topics. When this is the case, I simply create multiple groups focusing on that topic. In my experience, despite having the same topic, different groups will likely approach that topic from a different angle or discover different resources as they learn more about the selected topic with their group.

Random Grouping

Sometimes it is good to just randomly mix up the PSTs in the class. There are a variety of tools that can be used to mix PSTs into random groups. Some learning management systems have tools built in to create random groups, and there are also free online tools for this purpose. I use these occasionally, but I prefer to use and model strategies that my PSTs can carry into their classrooms regardless of the technology used in their school or district. Here are some of my favorite low-tech strategies:

a Hand a playing card to each PST as they enter the class. You can group students by suit (hearts, clubs, spades, diamonds), card number, color, and so on, depending on the number of groups you want to create. I often remove the face cards before doing this and may reduce the number of cards handed out based on the size of the class. Since playing cards are so versatile in terms of grouping, it is also difficult for students to "game" the system by switching cards.

b As students enter the classroom, they pick a button from a basket by the door. Then I direct students to group up by button color. I have found large buttons in single-color packs at craft stores and just put in the number of colors matching the number of groups I wish to make. The easy thing about this strategy is that you can put in the number of buttons to match the number of students and balance the size of the groups. This strategy can be used with any items that come in different colors, shapes, and so on. In some cases, I have added a little more incentive by using candy to make groups; different colors of Starburst or Dum Dums, for example, can be used to make groups. When I am making groups on the fly, I have just drawn symbols (squares, stars, circles, etc.) on sticky notes or popsicle sticks to form random groups.

c   Put words or sets of related words on index cards and have PSTs select a card as they enter the class. Students create groups by finding others with the same term or by finding others who have terms related to their word. For example, formative, summative, and diagnostic are all types of assessment, so PSTs with these terms would form one group, while behaviorism, constructivism, and cognitivism are all learning theories, so PSTs with these terms would form a different group.

Inviting Student Feedback

Being purposeful in inviting student feedback and transparent in utilizing this feedback is another way to create an environment in which PSTs feel comfortable taking risks, engaging in difficult discussions, and viewing the classroom as a space in which their perspectives are valued. It is important to acknowledge that, for many of the PSTs in your courses, this may be the first time they have been asked to give feedback *during* the course as opposed to simply completing course evaluations at the end of the semester (Whitehead, 2023). It is also important that students understand that your request for feedback is genuine and not intended to be a venue for fluffy compliments to butter up their instructor, nor will they be punished for providing constructive feedback.

Part of the process of inviting student feedback is discussing and modeling what useful, actionable feedback looks like. I often start by sharing some examples of feedback with PSTs and asking them to discuss which are the most useful and why. For examples that are less useful, we discuss what could be added to make them useful and actionable. This includes examples of both positive and constructive feedback. I use the term *constructive feedback* for feedback that suggests areas where change may be needed. This term reminds PSTs that such feedback should provide clarity on what can be built on (constructed) and removes the stigma of words such as *complaints* or *criticisms* for PSTs who aren't comfortable being critical of others, particularly their course instructors.

Examples of less useful feedback:

- Great class, thanks!

- I didn't like the quick write. It stressed me out!
- The group activity was boring.
- I liked today's discussion.

Examples of useful, actionable feedback:

- I appreciated that we had multiple opportunities to ask questions during class today. I am a lot less confused now!
- Only having 10 minutes to respond to the quick write didn't feel like enough time. I still had a lot more that I wanted to say.
- The jigsaw groups were helpful, but I think making the groups smaller would have given everyone more opportunities to participate.
- Today's discussion was engaging because we had time to hear different perspectives. It helped me think about the readings in a new way.

In sharing these examples, my PSTs and I discuss how the second set provides specific information on what worked or did not and why, which allows the instructor to consider adjustments to make for subsequent courses. I continue this conversation by making a connection to teacher feedback to students, with the goal of helping PSTs in my courses see these opportunities to provide feedback on my courses as additional practice in writing useful actionable feedback so that it becomes natural for them in their future teaching.

The strategies below can be completed on paper or can be completed utilizing technology tools such as online surveys, the university learning management system, and so on. I choose the format to utilize for each course based on the course modality and number of students. For larger courses, even those that are face-to-face, having students submit feedback online may make the process more efficient. In face-to-face courses where I also utilize the feedback tool to check attendance, a paper document tends to be more effective, as an online form may be filled out by students who were not actually present.

Conversation Calendar

The Conversation Calendar is a tool I have utilized in my work as a teacher educator for many years. It provides a venue for PSTs in my courses to give me feedback on my instruction and let me know what questions or confusion they may have after each class meeting. PSTs can respond to a sentence stem ("One of the most _____ things about class today was…"

with various adjectives to select from, including *interesting, meaningful, confusing, frustrating*) or just provide their own comments and questions. I occasionally provide more specific prompts, such as "How can I better support your growth as a future educator?" or "What questions do you still have after today's lesson?" As the instructor, I respond to each student's Conversation Calendar entry while also looking for themes across responses that can inform my instruction. Through this tool, I provide an opportunity for PSTs to share their feedback and feel heard by their instructor. When I make an adjustment to my instruction, I am transparent about the adjustment with my PSTs so that they know their voices have been heard. PSTs in my course appreciate the open communication the Conversation Calendar provides, as noted by the following quote from a final course evaluation:

> *I don't have much to say because I get to keep in constant communication with Sarah with the conversation calendar—a tool I think more teachers at [institution] should use. It is one thing to preach about being there for your students and caring about them but to have a tool like this to hold yourself accountable, I like it and I like how she models that for us as future teachers. —Course evaluation comment from a preservice teacher in K–8 ELA methods, fall 2018*

Stop, Start, Continue

This strategy asks PSTs to consider three prompts regarding the course: "What would you like the instructor to start doing?," "What would you like the instructor to stop doing?," and "What would you like the instructor to continue doing?" (Danley, 2019). I have adapted this to two sets of questions: one that considers the elements of the course controlled by the instructor and a second set that pushes PSTs to reflect on themselves and their impact on their own learning. The goal of this second set of questions is to support PSTs in taking ownership of their learning within the course. These questions can be answered through an exit ticket, open-ended survey, or any other format that works for collecting and utilizing the information. When I utilize this strategy, I often alternate the prompts between course meetings so that PSTs respond to instructor-focused questions after one meeting and personal reflection questions the next.

Instructor-Focused Questions:

What isn't helping to support your learning in this course and should be stopped?

What should your instructor start doing to support your learning in this course?

What is working well to support your learning in this course and should be continued?

PST Reflection Questions:

What habits or actions may be hindering your progress or participation in this course?

What new approaches or behaviors can you start adopting to enhance your own learning in this course?

What positive actions or strategies are you currently using that should be continued to support your success in this course?

Anonymous Feedback Cards

This strategy, adapted from Reeve et al. (2022), asks students to respond to a simple prompt on an index card at the end of class. No one is required to write anything if they have no feedback to share, but all are asked to turn in the card regardless of whether they have feedback. This allows students to submit feedback without feeling like they are in the spotlight. While Reeve and colleagues suggest the prompt "Any suggestions?," I have found more success with a specific prompt, such as "How can I better support your success in this course?" or "What do you need to meet the goals you have set for learning in this course?"

Reflection and Discussion Questions

"As a Teacher Educator" reflection questions are for the course instructor to reflect on their utilization of DI. "As a Learner" and "As an Educator" questions are for PSTs to reflect on their experience with differentiation as a learner and how they can apply that experience to their future classrooms. The two sets of questions consider the dual roles of PSTs in the teacher educator program. It is recommended that PSTs have an opportunity to reflect on these questions individually before sharing and discussing them with peers.

As a Teacher Educator:

1 How do you model and support risk-taking among the PSTs in the course?

2   How can you provide opportunities for PSTs in your courses to take ownership of their learning?

3   How can/do you use PST feedback to enhance sense of belonging and community within your classes?

4   What opportunities for collaboration and cocreation with PSTs can you leverage within your classes?

5   What classroom routines or strategies have you found to be most effective in maintaining consistency and predictability for PSTs in your courses without being too rigid?

6   What systems or tools can you implement to regularly collect and respond to feedback from PSTs in your courses?

7   Are there unintentional barriers in your classroom setup or interaction style that might marginalize some students? How can you adapt your practices to show future educators the importance of a universally welcoming learning space?

8   What adjustments can you make to ensure that students see the balance between giving learners autonomy and providing structure? How can you model the process of gradually releasing responsibility in a way that future educators can replicate?

9   How can you be more explicit about the relational strategies you use and why they are effective so that your future teachers have concrete examples to apply in their own practice?

As a Learner:

1   In what ways do you see your course instructor model and support risk-taking?

2   What specific aspects of the classroom environment help you feel safe and supported within this class?

3   How have you been given the opportunity to take ownership of your learning in this class?

4   How does having input on aspects of the classroom (such as due dates, rubrics, etc.) affect your learning and motivation?

5   How do different grouping strategies used within the class support you in collaborating effectively with your peers?

6   How do you feel about giving feedback to your instructor? Do you believe your suggestions are used to inform the instructor's practice?

7. Do you feel that your identity and experiences are valued within this class? How does this affect your learning, participation, and engagement?
8. How do different students in your current class respond to group work, and what might be some of the challenges that students from different cultural backgrounds, neurodiverse students, or students with different social backgrounds face in collaborative settings?

As an Educator

1. In what ways does giving students ownership over their learning (e.g., input on assignments, flexible deadlines) influence your engagement? How might you incorporate similar practices to empower students in your future teaching?
2. How do you plan to balance giving students autonomy with maintaining structure in your own classroom?
3. How do different grouping strategies in this class (e.g., flexible groups, Clock Buddies) support collaborative learning? What grouping techniques might you use in your future classroom to promote teamwork and peer learning?
4. How do you ensure that group work is meaningful and equitable, and what challenges might you face in implementing collaborative learning in your future classroom?
5. What factors in this classroom encourage you to take intellectual risks, and how can you create a similar environment in your future classroom where students feel comfortable taking risks and learning from mistakes?
6. How has your instructor's effort to build relationships with students (e.g., learning names, understanding interests) influenced your engagement in the classroom? How will you prioritize building relationships with your own students?
7. In this classroom, how does the teacher make space for diverse perspectives and cultural identities? How will you ensure that your future classroom is culturally responsive and inclusive?
8. What strategies will you use in your future classroom to create a flexible and comfortable physical space that meets the needs of all learners?

9 What specific tools or supports will you provide to help your students set realistic goals and reflect on their growth over time?

10 How could you adapt your approach to creating a safe environment to better support students who may face additional barriers (e.g., language learners, students with disabilities)?

11 How will you ensure that group work is both inclusive and equitable so that all students—regardless of their background or ability—can participate fully and benefit from the collaborative experience?

12 How will you adapt your teaching strategies to support students whose cultural or personal identities might not be represented in the mainstream curriculum or dominant school culture?

13 How might different students approach goal setting in your classroom, and how can you support students from various cultural or linguistic backgrounds in setting meaningful goals that reflect their personal and academic growth?

4 Differentiation by Content

Differentiation by content can be defined as adaptation and purposeful selection of the materials students are engaging with and of the methods utilized by the teacher to provide instruction (Jager et al., 2022). This aligns with the call of culturally responsive teaching (CRT) for teachers to select texts and instructional methods that are accessible and meaningful for their students while considering student knowledge and cultural background (Kieran & Anderson, 2019). Differentiation by content ensures that all learners have equitable access to materials that reflect their experiences and challenge them at appropriate levels. This process involves critically analyzing the resources used in the classroom. As part of this, teacher educators should consider questions such as "What contexts are included, and what contexts are missing?" or "Whose experiences or voices are not considered?" when selecting materials. Addressing these gaps means actively seeking out resources that incorporate diverse perspectives, ensuring that underrepresented voices are included. For example, when teaching preservice teachers (PSTs) about literacy instruction, the instructor might select case studies that highlight best practices for teaching multilingual learners or students with learning differences rather than focusing solely on traditional monolingual, Eurocentric, and neurotypical students.

Materials considered for differentiation extend beyond traditional textbooks to include multimedia resources, case studies, and real-world applications. For example, in a history education course, instead of relying on a single textbook, the instructor might provide access to primary source documents, oral histories, and contemporary narratives to allow PSTs to critically examine historical events from multiple perspectives. In a mathematics education course, PSTs might have access to mathematics problem-solving software, interactive simulations, demonstration videos that model utilization of manipulatives, and problem-based learning scenarios to explore various approaches to mathematics problem-solving.

Differentiation by content also applies to preparatory work before class meetings. PSTs might be given options for engaging with the material, such as reading a scholarly article, watching a documentary, or listening to a podcast on the topic. This ensures that students with different learning preferences or accessibility needs can process information in ways that are most effective for them. Additionally, incorporating a variety of sources encourages exposure to diverse perspectives, reinforcing the importance of critical analysis and multiple viewpoints in the learning process.

Content differentiation pushes educators to consider what specific materials students will engage with to support them in learning the content and skills necessary to meet proficiency in a given standard or learning outcome. To accomplish this, the educator needs to know students' starting points using pre-assessments or other measures. This knowledge provides opportunities to identify the areas students need to build foundation skills and knowledge as well as areas in which students may be ready for additional challenges.

By intentionally adapting content, teacher educators can model for PSTs how to make thoughtful instructional decisions that reflect the diverse needs of K–12 students. This not only enhances the learning experience for PSTs but also prepares them to create inclusive and equitable classrooms in their future teaching careers.

Strategies for Differentiating by Content: Materials

Providing Different Texts on the Same Topic

Often, there are multiple texts available on a specific topic, each offering differing perspectives or levels of complexity. Providing multiple texts that students can either choose from or that are purposefully assigned is one strategy that can be utilized to support student learning. In teacher education, this could include a research article and a practitioner-focused article based on the same work or a blog post from a professional organization that provides an overview of the work, including classroom applications and discussion points relevant to educators. Including texts in multiple modalities (see below) is another strategy for providing students with multiple access points for course content.

Providing Content in Multiple Formats/Modalities

Another strategy for differentiating content that builds on the previous suggestion is to provide the same content in multiple formats or modalities. For example, students may choose to engage with new information before a class discussion by reading a journal article, listening to the journal article using a text-to-speech tool, or listening to a podcast featuring the author of the article discussing the work. Additional text choices, such as infographics and videos, can also be included as options for students to engage with content. Through these various modalities, all PSTs in the course have access to the information but can engage with it in the ways that best fit their needs. This not only fosters a more inclusive learning environment but also allows for greater flexibility in how students manage their time and learning pace.

In many cases, I have had PSTs choose to read the initial article and then listen to the accompanying podcast (or vice versa) to strengthen and confirm their understanding of the information presented. Additionally, I've found that some PSTs prefer to review visual resources like infographics before diving into text-based content, as these visuals often provide a helpful conceptual overview. I have also had PSTs comment that audio options such as podcasts are helpful, as they can listen to them while driving or working out at the gym, times when they otherwise would not be able to engage with course materials. This flexibility is especially beneficial for those balancing work, family, and study commitments, as it offers multiple entry points for engaging with content on their own terms.

Adjusting Content Presented

After a pre-assessment, PSTs can be assigned content on foundational topics they have not yet mastered, allowing for a more efficient and targeted learning experience. This approach ensures that PSTs are neither overwhelmed with information they are not ready for nor required to review material they have already mastered.

For example, in a course on instructional strategies, a pre-assessment might gauge PSTs' familiarity with key pedagogical terms, such as *scaffolding*, *formative assessment*, and *differentiation*. PSTs who demonstrate proficiency in most of these terms would be assigned content on only the vocabulary they have not yet mastered. These PSTs could then engage with deeper readings, case studies, or reflective application exercises, such as analyzing a lesson plan to identify where and how scaffolding techniques are used. Meanwhile, those who need reinforcement on fundamental concepts would be provided with targeted readings, videos, or interactive activities to help them build a solid foundation before progressing to higher-order applications.

This approach allows for utilization of strategies such as compacting, in which PSTs engage only with the content or skills with which they have not already demonstrated proficiency. In addition, this allows the instructor to identify areas in which all PSTs in the course have strong background knowledge, providing an opportunity to reduce redundancy and instead build on topics to push higher levels of application, evaluation, and other critical thinking skills. For example, if a pre-assessment in a literacy instruction course reveals that all students have a strong grasp of phonemic awareness, the instructor can allocate more time to more complex topics, such as strategies for teaching phonemic awareness to various student populations, such as English language learners or students with language-processing challenges.

Strategies for Differentiating by Content: Methods

Providing a Summary or Guided Notes of the Content

Providing a summary or guided notes for students to utilize as a guide during lectures is a common accommodation for PSTs in my courses who are neurodiverse. Making these tools available for any students who could benefit from them is another step toward creating a classroom environment in which all PSTs have what they need to be successful. This can be as simple as making a student version of the presentation in which important terms are replaced with blanks for students to fill in during class or providing a guide with headings of the major topics to be covered. I usually provide these ahead of class time through the class learning management system. PSTs in my courses can choose whether to use these tools. When I notice a PST in my course who seems to be struggling, I check in and ask if they have been using the guided notes posted for each class meeting. If they have not, then doing so is one of my first recommendations. In the following guided notes example, the lesson introduces morphemes in an emergent literacy course for elementary PSTs. These guided notes include blanks for PSTs to fill in with information and examples from the lecture.

Example Guided Notes with Answer Key
Slide 1: Introduction to Morphemes
– A morpheme is the smallest unit of meaning in language.
– When we speak, morphemes are made up of _____ (sounds).
– When we write, morphemes are made of _____ (symbols).
– Unlike phonemes and graphemes, morphemes _____ (do/do not) carry meaning individually.
Types of Morphemes
Slide 3: Free Morphemes
– Free morphemes can function as words independently.
– Examples: _____, _____
– They can also be combined with other morphemes (e.g., _____, _____).
Slide 4: Bound Morphemes
- Bound morphemes cannot stand alone and must be attached to other morphemes.
– Examples include:
– Prefixes: _____, _____
– Suffixes: _____, _____, _____
– Some root words (e.g., _____, _____, _____)
Slide 7: Recognizing Free and Bound Morphemes
– Don't confuse syllables with morphemes. A morpheme can be one syllable or many. The focus is on the _____ carried.
– Example of a free morpheme: The word _____ (three syllables) is a free morpheme.

Answer key:
Introduction to Morphemes: phonemes; graphemes; do
Free Morphemes: book, run; bookcase, runner
Bound Morphemes: pre-, sub-; -ed, -tion, -ology; -ject (throw), bio- (life), aqua- (water)
Recognizing free and bound morphemes: meaning; elephant

Small-Group Instruction or Scaffolding

Grouping students based on their needs is a helpful strategy for supporting students who may need additional instructional support while providing opportunities for those who are ready for more challenge in content with which they have already shown proficiency to do so independently or collaboratively. For example, in an emergent literacy course I sometimes teach, some PSTs often need additional support in identifying the number of phonemes (sounds) in words, while other PSTs grasp this more quickly. On these occasions, I provide an application activity for PSTs who have reached proficiency in this skill, such as a premade lesson plan or instructional activity for them to analyze while I work with the PSTs who need more support identifying phonemes through guided practice.

Student Research

Providing students with opportunities to research topics independently or in collaborative groups instead of having content solely delivered by the instructor supports student ownership of their learning and can increase engagement. Within my TEP courses, I often do this through professional learning community (PLC) groups. To set up these groups, I provide PSTs with a list of topics to choose from and ask them to indicate the three topics they are most interested in, ranked from first to third. I use this information to create PLC groups of four or five PSTs based on their interest in a specific topic, creating multiple groups for a single topic if needed. I give each group a starting resource to provide some foundational information on their topic, after which they are responsible for finding additional reputable resources to read and discuss as a group, with a roundtable presentation to their peers in class at the end of the semester.

Technology Affordances/Tools

As a middle school English language arts teacher, I often used audiobooks as a tool for students who needed additional support when reading texts in my class when possible. Providing an audio version allowed students to access the material in a way that accommodated diverse learning needs, including those related to reading fluency, comprehension, or processing challenges. However, an audio version was not always available for every text, limiting this option.

Since I left the middle school classroom, new tools have become more readily available, and most electronic devices now come with built-in text-to-speech and speech-to-text capabilities, expanding accessibility for all learners. In my teacher education courses, PSTs are encouraged to utilize text-to-speech tools and other technology-based supports to enhance their engagement with and understanding of course materials. Additionally, transcripts of videos used in class are provided, which many PSTs find beneficial for note-taking and comprehension. This allows them to review content at their own pace, revisit key points, and engage with materials in multiple modalities.

Beyond text-to-speech, PSTs are encouraged to explore and experiment with other technological affordances that can aid in comprehension and engagement. This might include using annotation tools like Hypothesis for collaborative text discussions, interactive e-books that allow for embedded multimedia elements, or AI-powered summarization tools to help break down complex readings. For PSTs preparing to teach in digital or blended learning environments, these tools not only enhance their own learning but also serve as models for how they can implement similar strategies in their future classrooms to support accessibility and differentiated instruction (DI).

Strategies for Content Differentiation and More

The two tools in this section provide opportunities for differentiation by content but also cross over into both process and product differentiation. I am including them here due to the opportunities they offer for content differentiation but will refer to them in later chapters as well.

Task Charts

Task charts are a tool that provides individuals or groups of students with a specific rotation or list of activities based on their current level of knowledge and skill and the lesson learning goals (see Table 9). For example, the instructor may group students based on the results of a formative assessment, with groups working through a list of four activities to engage in out of a total of six to eight activities going on within the class. I typically use an acronym when naming groups to avoid implying proficiency levels within the naming of groups. My university is the Bobcats, so "Go Cats!" is a typical group-naming convention in my courses. Depending on the

Table 9 Example Task Chart

Learning goal: Identify and analyze key social, privacy, and ethical issues related to the use of technology in the classroom.

Task	Round 1: Monday, 10:10–10:30	Round 2: Monday, 10:30–10:50	Round 3: Wednesday, 10:05–10:25	Round 4: Wednesday, 10:25–10:45
Collaborative read-and-discuss	Group G	Group O	Group T	Group A
Instructor Q&A	Group O		Group G	
Case study analysis	Group C	Group G	Group O	Group T
EULA (end-user license agreement) audit	Group A	Group T	Group C	Group G
School policy review	Group T	Group C	Group A	Group O
Parent communication plan		Group A		Group C

space available in your classroom, students may physically move from one station to the next or may simply retrieve the materials for the next task (either physical materials or digital) and move on to that activity. Task charts can also cover more than a single class meeting. These activities may include a mix of engagement with new materials that cover content in various modalities, tasks to complete while engaging with the materials to support understanding, and short assessments to gauge student growth in understanding or skill.

The example task chart (Table 9) is set up to cover two class meetings in a class that meets for 50 minutes twice per week (10:00 to 10:50 a.m.). The example schedule allows time for an introduction of the activity on the first day from 10:00 to 10:10 and a brief reminder of expectations on the second day from 10:00 to 10:05 with a brief whole-class wrap-up on the second day from 10:45 to 10:50. The tasks are selected to align with the stated learning outcome regarding technology use in the classroom:

- The collaborative read-and-discuss asks PSTs to read a short article about privacy concerns and technology use in education and provides a series of questions to guide the group in discussion. Guiding questions may include the following:
  - What federal laws are relevant to the integration of technology in education and students' data privacy?
  - What are some of the privacy risks associated with technology use in schools?
  - What policies or practices should teachers be aware of when utilizing educational technology?
  - How might privacy concerns related to technology differ by student age level?
  - How can teachers balance the benefits of instructional technology with student privacy rights?
- The instructor Q&A is a small-group discussion with the instructor in which PSTs have a chance to ask clarifying questions on the topic and the instructor provides an additional targeted mini lecture if needed. This specific task is usually targeted at PSTs who need additional support with the topic or those who have a lot of questions that can be best addressed in this format. The Q&A may begin with some targeted questions from the instructor to begin the discussion or

with an opportunity for PSTs to write down questions they have and prioritize them to make sure their most pressing questions are discussed.
- The case study analysis engages PSTs in analyzing a classroom situation and developing a plan to address the scenario either individually or in collaboration with their peers in the group. The case study analysis can include prompts or questions to guide PSTs as they consider the situation presented in the case study. For example, if PSTs are analyzing a case study in which a teacher is using a third-party app to track student behavior and a parent raises a concern about data security, guiding prompts could include the following:
  - What are the ethical and legal concerns within this case study?
  - What steps should the teacher take to ensure that student data within the app are secure?
  - What proactive steps could the teacher have taken to avoid this concern?
  - Imagine you are the teacher in this scenario and you need to communicate the situation to your principal. Write an e-mail in which you explain your perspective on the situation, including your rationale for using the app, or, with a peer, role-play a conversation between the teacher and the principal, discussing the situation and exploring possible solutions.
- The end-user license agreement (EULA) audit pushes PSTs to read the fine print they agree to when signing up for an educational technology tool and, using a series of prompts, consider any potential privacy or other concerns.
  - What data will the tool be collecting from the teacher? From students?
  - Who owns the data?
  - How are the data stored?
  - How transparent is the company about how collected data are used?
  - Are there any terms within the EULA that raise privacy concerns for students, teachers and schools, or parents?
- For the school policy review, PSTs read the educational technology policy for a local school district and write a reflection regarding what a new teacher in the district needs to know about the policy and what questions a new teacher might have after reading the policy.

This reflection will be guided by a series of questions, such as the following:
- What is the policy for technology use by teachers/within classrooms in this district?
- Describe any approval process for the utilization of new technology, such as apps or subscription websites, within classrooms in this district.
- What responsibilities do teachers have for protecting student privacy within this district's policy?
- Discuss any areas in which the policy seems outdated.
- Discuss any areas in which the policy is unclear.
- What questions might a teacher who is new to the district have after reviewing this policy?

- The parent communication plan asks PSTs to take what they have learned about student privacy and ethical use of electronic communication with parents and caregivers and create a plan for their future classroom addressing how they will communicate with students' families regarding their progress while following guidelines to protect student privacy and maintain ethical communication practices. This will include methods they will use to communicate with parents, how they will address and protect student privacy when utilizing each of the selected methods, and sample communications to demonstrate professional communication skills and the understanding of student privacy.

Learning Contracts

Learning contracts are collaborative agreements between the teacher and student regarding how the student will work toward proficiency during a stated time period. As such, it often includes elements of content, product, and process differentiation. While learning contracts can be done one-on-one with students (aligning more with personalized instruction), I have created contracts that serve as more of a checklist from which PSTs select from a menu of options (see Table 10). Thus, there are some nonnegotiables within the contract that apply to all PSTs within the course, while there will be other areas in which PSTs select options that work best for them. In the example below, Choice Set 1 provides an opportunity for content differentiation through two curated resources (one podcast and one video) and provides

Table 10 Example Learning Contract

Educational Psychology Module 1
Learning ContractInstructor name:
PST name:
Date:
Course Learning Outcomes:

- Explain major learning theories, such as behaviorism, cognitivism, constructivism, and social learning theory.
- Identify the key principles and applications of each learning theory in different educational contexts.

The purpose of this learning contract is to outline the expectations and commitments for your engagement in the first module of this course. It is designed to help you set goals and demonstrate proficiency in the above learning outcomes.

Required Components (for all PSTs)	Due Date	Completed
Read Chapter 1 in textbook	Meeting 2	
Read Chapters 2–3 in textbook	Meeting 3	
Read Chapters 4–5 in textbook	Meeting 4	
Complete Comparison Chart of Learning Theories	Meeting 4	
Engage in class activities and discussions	Ongoing	
Module 1 Quiz	Meeting 7	
Choice Set 1: Choose one from this category			

Check Option Chosen	Option	Due Date	Completed
	Listen to the podcast linked in Module 1 and create a graphic organizer or make notes to identify important points and connections to course readings.	Meeting 4	
	View the learning theories video linked in Module 1 and create a graphic organizer or make notes to identify important points and connections to course readings.		

	Find an additional reputable resource about learning theories and create a graphic organizer or make notes to identify important points and connections to course readings.		
\multicolumn{4}{c}{Choice Set 2: Choose one from this category}			
Check Option Chosen	**Option**	**Due Date**	**Completed**
	Observe a classroom and analyze the instructional strategies used. Identify which learning theories are evident in the teacher's practices. Write a report discussing how behaviorism, cognitivism, constructivism, and/or social learning theory are being applied and how effective they are in supporting student learning.	Meeting 6	
	Create a case study based on a specific educational scenario (e.g., a classroom struggling with engagement, a student with special needs). Identify how at least two of the learning theories (behaviorism, cognitivism, constructivism, and social learning theory) would be applied in this context to improve student outcomes.		

	Choice Set 2: Choose one from this category		
Check Option Chosen	**Option**	**Due Date**	**Completed**
	Outline a brief lesson plan (15–30 minutes) aimed at teaching a specific concept or skill in a content area and grade level of your choice. In the lesson plan, incorporate at least *two* of the following learning theories: behaviorism, cognitivism, constructivism, or social learning theory. Afterward, write a short reflection on how the chosen theories influenced your lesson design and how they could impact student learning.		

By signing this contract, I agree to meet the expectations outlined in this document in order to fulfill the requirements of Module 1 in this course. I understand that failure to complete these requirements will impact my grade. I also acknowledge that the quality of work completed will also be considered in determining my success (and grade) in this module.

Student signature:
Date:
Instructor signature:
Date:

PSTs with an opportunity to find a resource on their own while providing two strategies for process differentiation (graphic organizer or notes). Learning contracts also provide an additional opportunity for PSTs to engage in goal setting (see Chapter 2) and reflect on their progress toward these goals.

Reflection and Discussion Questions

"As a Teacher Educator" reflection questions are for the course instructor to reflect on their utilization of DI. "As a Learner" and "As an Educator" questions are for PSTs to reflect on their experience with differentiation as a learner and how they can apply that experience to their future classrooms. The two sets of questions consider the dual roles of PSTs in the teacher educator program. It is recommended that PSTs have an opportunity to reflect on these questions individually before sharing and discussing them with peers.

As a Teacher Educator:

1. How do I currently determine my students' starting points before beginning a unit or topic? What pre-assessment methods could I incorporate to gain better insights into their prior knowledge and skills? (See Chapter 2 for pre-assessment strategies.)
2. How do I identify students who need additional foundational support versus those ready for more advanced challenges?
3. How do I decide which materials or resources are most appropriate for my students' varying needs?
4. How can I integrate culturally responsive texts and methods into my content selection process?
5. How might I provide multiple texts on the same topic in my courses? What resources could I use to ensure a balance between academic rigor and accessibility?
6. What technology affordances or tools could enhance my ability to differentiate instruction by content and method?
7. How do I ensure that my differentiated materials and methods are culturally responsive and inclusive of my students' diverse backgrounds?
8. How will I assess the effectiveness of my differentiated strategies? What indicators will show that these adjustments are supporting student learning and engagement?

As a Learner:

1. How did having access to different types of materials (e.g., texts, podcasts, and infographics) on the same topic impact your understanding and engagement with the content?
2. When you were assigned content tailored to your prior knowledge or skill level, how did it affect your learning process and motivation?

3. How did using a task chart or learning contract impact your ability to focus on learning goals? Did you feel these tools helped you meet the learning outcomes effectively?
4. How did small-group instruction based on skill levels or needs affect your learning and engagement? How did it impact your interactions with peers?
5. How did your peers experience the differentiation strategies utilized? Did their experiences align with or differ from yours? What insights can you gain from their perspectives?
6. Did you find that the materials or methods selected by your instructor aligned with your cultural knowledge or background? How did this alignment (or lack of alignment) influence your engagement?
7. Which differentiation strategies did you find most effective for your learning, and why? Were there any strategies that felt less effective or challenging for you?
8. In what ways did the instructor's choice of texts or instructional methods reflect culturally responsive teaching? How did this modeling help you understand how to make content accessible and meaningful for diverse learners?
9. How did the instructor balance providing foundational support for some students while challenging others with more advanced tasks? What lessons can you take from these decisions for your own classroom?
10. In what ways did the instructor's methods (e.g., guided notes, technology tools, and small groups) serve as a practical example of differentiation? How might these methods inform your teaching strategies?

As an Educator:

1. How did experiencing these differentiation strategies influence your understanding of how to apply them in your own future teaching practice?
2. How will you ensure that the content and methods you choose in your future classroom are accessible and culturally responsive for all students?

3. How do you think technology tools used for differentiation (e.g., text-to-speech tools and multimedia formats) supported or hindered your learning? How might you use these tools in your future classroom?
4. How will you ensure that your differentiation strategies support students who need foundational skill building while also challenging those who are ready to go deeper?
5. What strategies will you use to offer your students choices in how they engage with content, and how will you ensure that all options are meaningful and aligned with learning goals?
6. How might tools like task charts or learning contracts help you organize and manage DI in your classroom? What adjustments would you make to fit the age-group and subject you plan to teach?
7. How will you create opportunities for students to take ownership of their learning, such as selecting texts, identifying learning goals, or contributing to learning contracts?
8. How will you create or curate materials in multiple formats (e.g., texts, podcasts, and infographics) to ensure accessibility and engagement for all students?
9. How will you assess the success of your differentiation strategies? What specific indicators will you look for to determine if your approach is meeting students' needs?

5 Differentiation by Process

Differentiation by process can be defined as varying the ways in which students engage with and make sense of course materials. Differentiating instruction by process, as with any other type of differentiation, requires a knowledge of the students in the class and their learning needs. This level of differentiation can be achieved through several strategies, including student choice, purposeful grouping, and scaffolding, all of which are supportive of student success and agency. For example, student choice allows learners to engage with content in ways that align with their interests and strengths. A teacher might offer multiple activities for exploring a historical event, such as analyzing primary sources, watching a documentary, or participating in a debate, allowing students to select the method they feel best supports their learning. Scaffolding strategies help ensure that all students can access and engage with the material. A teacher might provide sentence stems or graphic organizers to support students in writing a persuasive essay or use guided questioning to help students break down a complex math problem.

Additionally, differentiation by process includes opportunities for students to practice skills at their own pace. One example is station-based learning, where preservice teachers (PSTs) rotate through activities targeting different skills related to lesson planning. One station may focus on aligning objectives with standards, another on selecting appropriate instructional strategies, and another on assessing student learning. This method allows PSTs to engage with each component at their own level, seeking additional support where needed or moving ahead to more complex applications when ready.

Finally, extension opportunities are essential for students who are ready to deepen their understanding. In a course on classroom management, for example, PSTs who quickly grasp basic strategies could be challenged to analyze real classroom scenarios, identifying potential behavior management interventions and justifying their choices based on educational theory. Similarly, in a literacy instruction course, PSTs who show proficiency in designing differentiated reading lessons might be asked to develop a professional development session for peers on best practices for supporting struggling readers.

Differentiating by content and differentiation by process often go hand in hand, and delineating the two can sometimes be a challenge. Differentiation by content focuses more on the materials and direct instruction methods being utilized, while process differentiation focuses more on how students are engaging with the material. Due to the nature of these two types of differentiation, you will notice some overlap in the strategies included within the two chapters on these specific areas of differentiation. Process differentiation can also overlap with product differentiation, as students are often completing products as they are engaging with content. For purposes of this chapter, I will focus on strategies that may lead to or support student success in creating products or strategies that serve as informal assessments, and in the following chapter, I will focus on tasks that serve primarily as more formal formative or summative assessments of knowledge and skills.

Strategies for Differentiation by Process

General Strategies

Give Steps One to Three at a Time

One thing I have noticed as a teacher both in middle school and at the college level is that my students often forget the directions that have been shared about halfway through a task or activity. Based on Cognitive Load Theory (Sweller, 1988), this could be due to high demand on their working memory, which can hold between five and nine chunks of information at any time for neurotypical individuals. For neurodivergent individuals who have working memory challenges, including those with attention deficit hyperactivity disorder and autism spectrum disorder, fewer chunks of information can be retained in the working memory at any given time (Kofler et al., 2020; Wang et al., 2017). Providing steps for complicated tasks a few at a time or providing them in a readily accessible step-by-step format that students can refer to can help prevent cognitive overload and support students in completing the task successfully. In addition, this can also reduce the number of times directions need to be repeated. It is also important to remember that even a seemingly simple task may have multiple steps that we (instructors) are assuming students innately know and will remember. For example, when assigning students to write a summary of an article, we may assume that they automatically know the necessary steps. However, this task actually involves multiple actions: identifying key points in the text, organizing those points into a logical sequence, paraphrasing information in their own words, and ensuring that their summary is concise yet complete. Without explicit guidance, some students may struggle with one or more of these steps, leading to frustration or incomplete work. Providing a checklist, graphic organizer, or model examples can help students break the task down and complete it more successfully.

Create a Checklist for Major Tasks

When faced with a complex or multistep task, some of my PSTs reported feeling overwhelmed and, due to this, avoided getting started. To help them get started with confidence, I introduce them to the Major Assignment Steps Checklist (Table 11). This tool helps them break the assignment into more manageable chunks, set goal deadlines for completing each chunk, and keep track of their progress. By visually mapping out their work, PSTs can develop stronger time management and executive functioning skills—critical competencies for both their academic success and their future roles as educators.

I also provide a space for them to include opportunities for progress checks. Some PSTs prefer to schedule regular check-ins with me, where we review their progress, troubleshoot challenges, and make adjustments as needed. Others choose an accountability buddy within the class, meeting periodically to support each other, exchange feedback, and stay on track. These peer check-ins not only help students stay accountable but also create a collaborative learning environment where PSTs can share insights and solve problems together.

The checklist also encourages backward mapping from the final due date, helping PSTs plan strategically so that they make consistent progress instead of cramming everything into the last few days before submission. Backward mapping is a structured planning strategy that promotes time management and goal setting. In this approach, the PST starts with the assignment due date and works backward to determine steps to assignment completion

Table 11 Example Major Assignment Steps Checklist

Directions: The following checklist can help you keep track of the steps of your major project for this course. Utilizing this checklist, you can set your own goal due dates for each section of the assignment, keep track of your progress, and schedule check-ins with your instructor or accountability buddy.

Assignment Step	Assignment Due Date: XX/XX/XXXX				
	Completion Goal	Progress Check	Progress Check	Progress Check	Progress Check
Step 1: Choose a topic for text set	XX/XX				
Step 2: Select grade level for unit	XX/XX				
Step 3: Select and analyze 5–10 texts for text set	XX/XX				
Step 4: Plan unit assessment(s)	XX/XX				
Step 5: Plan lesson 1	XX/XX				
Step 6: Plan lesson 2	XX/XX				
Step 7: Plan lesson 3	XX/XX				
Step 8: Plan lesson 4	XX/XX				
Step 9: Check scaffolding and differentiation in all lessons	XX/XX				
Step 10: Check lesson plan template for all lessons	XX/XX				
Step 11: Proofreading and edits	XX/XX				
Step 12: Submit final assignment	XX/XX				

by identifying key milestones, estimating the time needed for each step, and setting deadlines for incremental progress. This method allows PSTs to create a realistic timeline for completing each step, ensuring adequate time for research, drafting, revising, and seeking feedback if necessary. By setting smaller, more achievable deadlines, students can spread their workload evenly, reducing stress and increasing the likelihood of producing high-quality work. For example, in a unit-planning assignment, students might break the task into sections such as selecting learning objectives, designing activities, creating assessments, and writing reflections. Rather than attempting to complete the entire unit plan in one sitting, they can set goal deadlines for each stage, ensuring that they have adequate time for revision and feedback.

Additionally, I encourage PSTs to customize the checklist based on their individual needs and organizational approach. Some prefer to include specific reminders, such as "schedule library research session" or "draft introduction paragraph by Wednesday." Others may use color coding to visually differentiate between assignment steps that they have completed and those that still need attention. For larger projects, such as action research projects or instructional design portfolios, PSTs can even expand the checklist to include space for notes, reflections, or questions to discuss during check-ins.

Front-Load Vocabulary or Concepts before the Lesson

Pre-assessments such as the vocabulary chart or mind map (see Chapter 2) can provide information regarding the specific vocabulary or concepts central to a lesson or module and provide insight into students' knowledge of these before instruction. These assessments not only help instructors gauge what PSTs already know but also identify gaps that may need to be addressed before students engage with more complex material. Based on pre-assessment results, the teacher can front-load essential concepts and vocabulary, ensuring that all students have a foundational understanding before diving deeper into the lesson.

One effective way to front-load information is through multimodal resources, such as videos or podcasts that PSTs watch or listen to before class. These resources provide a preview of essential terms and ideas, allowing students to come to class better prepared to engage in discussions, activities, and higher-order thinking tasks. For example, before introducing a unit on assessment types in education, I might create a short video explaining key terms, such as *formative assessment*, *summative assessment*, *criterion-referenced assessment*, *norm-referenced assessment*, and *authentic assessment*. PSTs who are unfamiliar with these terms can review the material at their own pace, while those with prior knowledge can use the resource as reinforcement.

I create many videos for my courses because they offer both instructional and logistical advantages. As an instructor, once I have developed a video introducing important terms and concepts, I can reuse and adapt it in future semesters, cutting down on preparation time while maintaining quality instruction. Additionally, these videos allow for greater flexibility, as PSTs can watch them at their convenience, pausing, rewinding, or rewatching them as needed to reinforce their understanding.

My students have consistently expressed that these videos are particularly helpful for review. Many have shared that they revisit them when completing assignments, studying for exams, or preparing for class discussions. Recognizing this, I also provide video transcripts as note-taking support, ensuring that students who need written reinforcement can engage with the content in a format that works best for them. Some PSTs use the transcript to highlight key terms, create flash cards, or summarize the material in their own words—strategies that support retention and comprehension.

At the request of former students, I have uploaded select videos to a platform they can access even after completing my course so that they can review them while preparing for their licensure exams. This has been especially beneficial for students studying for assessments such as the Praxis or edTPA. Additionally, some PSTs have shared that they have used these videos as teaching resources in their early field experiences, referring back to them while planning lessons or assisting K–12 students.

Beyond video content, other front-loading strategies can also support diverse learners. A short lecture at the start of class, a graphic organizer outlining key concepts, or a collaborative word wall where students contribute definitions and examples can help reinforce important vocabulary. In many courses, I have also used interactive vocabulary games, including digital flash card platforms like Quizlet or Kahoot! to engage PSTs in a low-stakes, gamified review of terms. By systematically front-loading vocabulary and concepts, instructors can not only enhance student comprehension but also model instructional strategies that PSTs can later implement in their own classrooms.

Provide a Model of the Task

One statement I frequently make in my classes is "I won't ask you to do anything I have not done myself." In this spirit, I provide models of tasks to support PSTs as they engage with assignments that may be in an unfamiliar format (such as an exam blueprint or a new lesson plan template) or require multiple complex steps (such as a thematic unit plan or an action research project). Providing models helps PSTs visualize expectations, break down intimidating tasks into manageable parts, and develop confidence in their ability to complete the work successfully.

Along with these models, I often create video walk-throughs, where I guide students through the structure and content of the model while sharing insights into my thought process. These videos not only explain the task but also highlight key decision-making points, common pitfalls to avoid, and strategies for success. For example, when introducing a new lesson plan format, I might walk through a sample lesson I have written, explaining why I selected specific objectives, instructional strategies, and assessment methods. By verbalizing my approach, I make the implicit aspects of lesson planning explicit.

In addition to the model walk-through video, I also create a separate video that deconstructs the rubric for the assignment. In this video, I score the provided model, explaining how the rubric criteria align with expectations and demonstrating how different levels of performance would be assessed. PSTs have shared that this process clarifies what high-quality work looks like, helping them self-assess their own progress before submission. This practice is particularly valuable for students who are new to rubric-based assessment or have previously struggled with unclear grading expectations.

Beyond videos, I also encourage interactive engagement with models:

- Collaborative Model Analysis: Before assigning complex tasks such as an exam blueprint, I provide a completed sample and have PSTs work in small groups to analyze it using the rubric. PSTs discuss what makes the model effective and suggest potential improvements to better meet the rubric criteria.
- Partial Models: For tasks requiring significant creativity or autonomy, I provide partially completed models and have students brainstorm how they would complete the missing sections. I also make sure PSTs know that there is no one correct approach to completing the model task. This approach balances scaffolding with independent thinking.
- Comparative Models: When possible, I provide multiple models of varying quality levels and have PSTs work in groups to identify strengths and areas for improvement. This not only deepens their

understanding of the task but also enhances their ability to evaluate student work using a rubric or other criteria—a critical skill for future educators.

By incorporating models, video explanations, and rubric deconstructions, teacher educators can ensure that PSTs approach assignments with clarity and confidence. More important, this approach models effective instructional practices they can later use in their own classrooms—demonstrating how transparency, scaffolding, and metacognitive strategies support student success.

Decrease or Increase the Complexity of the Task

Differentiation by task complexity allows PSTs to engage with course content at a level that is appropriate to their background knowledge and skill level, ensuring that all students can access and apply new learning while also providing opportunities for challenge. By decreasing or increasing task complexity, instructors can tailor learning experiences to meet the diverse needs of their students while maintaining high expectations for all.

Case Studies

Case studies are a useful tool for engaging PSTs in considering situations they may encounter in the classroom, ranging from classroom management and instructional choices to communicating with caregivers. Case studies may be highly detailed with a lot of noise (additional information that may not be as relevant) or shorter and more to the point. As I select or create case studies for the PSTs in my courses, I consider their background knowledge and previous experiences applying that knowledge to the situations in the case studies. Based on that, how much noise will they be able to sort through? Are there some students who have already demonstrated the ability to engage in applying their knowledge critically and in thoughtful ways? With these questions in mind, I typically create two versions of any case studies I am using in class, with the second version including more noise, along with one different application or evaluation question to push students who are ready for more of a challenge. Below I include two versions of a case study that I created for a literacy assessment course to illustrate how I approach this strategy for differentiation. Example A is a shorter, less noisy version of the case study that includes only the most necessary information, while

Example B includes more irrelevant details and one additional question for PSTs to consider.

Example Case Study A:

It's the week before winter break, and Ms. Shannon's first-grade class has just completed their mid-year progress monitoring. Ms. Shannon is particularly concerned about Rey, who is reading significantly below benchmark. Progress monitoring indicates that Rey is able to decode consonant-vowel-consonant (CVC) words fluently but is inconsistent in decoding the more complex phonics patterns learned in class, such as words including "Magic e" or words with digraphs, such as "sh" and "ch." While Rey can easily sound out words like "cat" and "dog," words like "chip," "shop," and "bake" are often a challenge.

In addition, Rey's spelling of CVC words is inconsistent. Sometimes Rey spells "pen" correctly, but at other times, it comes out as "pan" or even "pein." However, the assessments used for progress monitoring do not provide any further details about the specific areas in which Rey needs additional instruction, and Rey's inconsistency in both decoding and spelling makes it difficult for Ms. Shannon to pinpoint areas in which Rey needs support.

For this case study, respond to the following prompts:

1. What specific information would be beneficial for Ms. Shannon to inform instruction and support for Rey? Why?
2. What assessment(s) would you recommend be utilized to provide this information? Support your response with a rationale for the use of the specific assessment(s).
3. What additional resources (materials, people, and so on) might Ms. Shannon need to utilize these assessments?

Example Case Study B:

It's the week before winter break, and excitement is buzzing in Ms. Shannon's first-grade classroom. Students are eagerly anticipating their holiday festivities, but in the midst of all the excitement, Ms. Shannon is deep in thought. She has just completed the mid-year progress monitoring for her class, and as she flips through the results, one student stands out—Rey. Ms. Shannon's eyes narrow in concern as she looks over the scores. Rey, who has been a quiet presence in the classroom, is significantly below the benchmark for reading, and Ms. Shannon knows that she needs to act soon. The report shows that Rey can decode CVC words fluently, but the progress is inconsistent beyond that phonics pattern. Rey has not yet shown any significant improvement in decoding more complex phonics patterns, which the class has been working on extensively in recent weeks. Rey is struggling with more complex phonics patterns, especially when it comes to digraphs and blends like "ch-" and "sh-" and other, similar phonics patterns, as well as the "Magic e." While Rey can easily sound out words like "cat" and "dog," words like "chip," "shop," and "bake" are often a challenge. These phonics patterns seem to trip Rey up most of the time.

To make matters more complicated, Rey's spelling of CVC words is inconsistent. Sometimes Rey spells "pen" correctly, but at other times, it comes out as "pan" or even "pein." However, the assessments used for progress monitoring do not provide any further details about the specific areas in which Rey needs additional instruction, and Rey's inconsistency in both decoding and spelling makes it difficult for Ms. Shannon to pinpoint areas in which Rey needs support. For example, the progress monitoring assessments show that Rey is below benchmark but do not indicate if Rey is struggling more with consonant blends, digraphs, vowel teams, or other phonics patterns. Ms. Shannon feels like she's missing a piece of the puzzle.

In the classroom, Rey has always been friendly and polite but has tended to fall behind during whole-group reading lessons. Rey participates in group activities, but there are signs of frustration when it comes to independent work, especially when faced with new or unfamiliar words. Rey's classmates seem to progress with little difficulty, and Ms. Shannon can't help but wonder if Rey might be falling through the cracks.

For this case study, respond to the following prompts:

1 What specific information would be beneficial for Ms. Shannon to inform instruction and support for Rey? Why?

2 What assessment(s) would you recommend be utilized to provide this information? Support your response with a rationale for the use of the specific assessment(s).

3 What additional resources (materials, people, and so on) might Ms. Shannon need to utilize these assessments?

4 If the results of the recommended assessments are still inconsistent or unclear in some other way, what next steps would you recommend for Ms. Shannon?

Tiered Activities

Tiered activities provide students with different ways to approach content at a level of challenge appropriate to their initial background knowledge, skill, and other readiness indicators (Sousa & Tomlinson, 2018). These activities provide all students with the opportunity to work toward proficiency in the identified content or skill while also acknowledging current levels of readiness.

Tiered Activity Example 1: For a learning outcome focused on the application of best practices for teaching number sense to early elementary students, PSTs could be provided with one of the following options based on their readiness:

Tier 1: Annotate a ready-made lesson plan to identify areas in which best practices are or are not being utilized, with references to class readings. In areas where best practices are not utilized, identify a best practice that could replace the current information.

Tier 2: Complete a partially completed lesson plan by adding best practices for teaching number sense in the identified sections, with references to class readings.

Tier 3: Given the standard, grade level, and assessment, create an instructional plan for teaching number sense using best practices, with references to class readings.

In this example, Tier 1 asks PSTs to identify best practices and practices that are not consistent with best practices and replace less optimal practices with best practices, while Tier 2 pushes PSTs to select best practices that align with the existing lesson plan elements with less supporting information. Tier 3 also engages PSTs in selection of best practices that align with the existing lesson but provides fewer complete elements within the existing lesson. All Tiers require that PSTs make connections to course readings to support the choices made regarding best practices. Through these tiered activities, all PSTs have an opportunity to engage in the identified learning outcome at a level that builds on their current skills and knowledge, with increasing complexity at each Tier.

Tiered Activity Example 2: For a learning outcome focused on the ethical use of technology in the K–12 classroom, PSTs can be provided with one of the following options based on their readiness:

Tier 1: Analyze an existing classroom scenario where technology is used inappropriately or unethically. This could include issues such as privacy violations, plagiarism, or misuse of online resources. After reviewing the scenario, identify ethical issues and recommend strategies for addressing them based on ethical guidelines for technology use (e.g., from ISTE Standards, FERPA, and so on).

Tier 2: Review a case study about the use of technology in a K–12 classroom, identifying ethical concerns related to digital privacy, security, or online behavior. Create a plan for how technology can be integrated into the lesson plan ethically, referencing specific ethical guidelines, policies, or legal regulations. The plan should include clear steps to address ethical dilemmas (e.g., ensuring student data privacy, preventing cyberbullying, promoting responsible digital citizenship).

Tier 3: Design a brief plan for integrating technology into a K–12 lesson while adhering to ethical guidelines. The plan should include two or three technology tools or resources, accompanied by a rationale for their use. In the plan, identify at least one ethical concern (e.g., student data privacy, equitable access to technology) and describe strategies for addressing it. The plan should also include one method for assessing students' understanding of ethical technology use.

In this second example, Tier 1 asks PSTs to identify and recommend solutions for ethical dilemmas within a given scenario, with a focus on recognizing problems. Tier 2 involves a more comprehensive review of a case study and the creation of a detailed, ethical plan for technology integration. Tier 3 pushes PSTs to create a comprehensive ethical technology integration plan for a classroom lesson, addressing potential ethical concerns and outlining strategies for teaching responsible technology use. These tiered activities ensure that all PSTs engage with the learning outcome in ways that build on their existing understanding while pushing them to expand their knowledge of ethical practices in technology use.

Modify the Number or Timing of Practice Opportunities
Adjust the Number of Practice Questions

Textbooks and other resources often organize end-of-chapter or unit review questions from easier to more difficult. This organization provides me, as the instructor, an opportunity to differentiate through assigning different questions to PSTs based on their assessment results and other observations during instruction. Thus, PSTs who have indicated a less solid understanding of the content in the chapter might be assigned the basic knowledge questions at the end of the chapter along with some application questions that build on this information. PSTs who have demonstrated a more concrete understanding of the basic information may be assigned fewer questions that require higher-order thinking (e.g., questions that require PSTs to apply the information, create new resources, or critique instructional materials). This can also be done by assigning only odd or even questions. If utilizing this strategy, pay attention to what answers, if any, are provided within the textbook. Many textbooks and similar resources provide answers only to odd-numbered questions in the student version of the textbook. I have taken advantage of this by assigning odd-numbered questions to PSTs who may need additional support, allowing them to check their answers and gain confidence as they work through the problems. Meanwhile, I assign the even-numbered questions to PSTs ready for more independent practice.

Flexible Pacing

Let PSTs engage in practice tasks until they reach proficiency, regardless of how quickly or slowly that happens. This can be achieved through structured opportunities for revision and self-paced learning elements. For example, instructors can build in multiple submission opportunities for key assignments, allowing PSTs to receive feedback and revise their work to demonstrate progress toward proficiency. Additionally, asynchronous learning modules with interactive practice tasks, such as discussion boards, quizzes with unlimited attempts, or case study analyses, can provide PSTs with the ability to progress at their own speed while still adhering to overall course deadlines. One specific tool I utilize in my courses is course videos with built-in quizzes that require a minimum score before the next section of the module in the learning management system opens for each student. By requiring a minimum score and allowing for multiple opportunities to watch the video and take the embedded quiz, students can engage with the material as many times as necessary to master the content.

Another approach is to use tiered assignment due dates or soft deadlines, where PSTs must complete foundational tasks before moving on to more advanced applications. For example, in a literacy assessment course, PSTs might first complete a scaffolded practice analysis of a student reading sample before applying the same process independently to a more complex assessment. Those who demonstrate proficiency quickly can move on, while those who do not receive additional support and opportunities for practice.

Specific Strategies and Tools
Jigsaw Activity (aka Expert Groups)

There are multiple approaches to a jigsaw or expert group activity. This section will discuss two potential models. Both involve students working in small groups, with each group assigned a specific topic or section of a text. The groups are working together to become experts on their specific topic/text. In the first model, each group creates a presentation or visual they utilize to share the main points of their topic/text with the entire class. The second model requires the students to be regrouped into new groups that include one person from each of the original groups. Students then take turns sharing main points from their topic/text with their new group. At the end of this process, each group works together to synthesize the information learned. One of the strengths of the second jigsaw strategy is the peer teaching aspect, which actively engages all students in both teaching and learning throughout the activity. Research has shown that the jigsaw strategy to increase both student engagement and knowledge of their focus topic (Dnyanesh et al., 2022) and for PSTs specifically has a significant effect on science learning outcomes (Mukaghiana et al., 2022).

I have also combined the jigsaw strategy with a *gallery walk* when I am in a classroom that has space for PSTs to move around. When combining these two approaches, I have each group create a visual to share the important information from their reading on a large piece of chart paper or a whiteboard and then hang these up around the room. Then new groups are formed that have one person from each expert group. Each newly formed group starts at a different visual. The individual within the gallery walk group who helped create that visual explains it to their new group and answers any clarifying questions. After a certain time, I give the students a signal to rotate clockwise to the next visual. Rotations repeat until all groups have had an opportunity to learn from each visual. One of the aspects of this adaptation, as well as the second format of the jigsaw mentioned in the previous paragraph, that I appreciate is that all group members know they will be accountable for explaining their group's information to peers, so there is less likelihood that one or two people will do all the work in a group while the others disengage.

Graphic Organizers

Graphic organizers are useful tools for helping students organize information as they are engaging with content. There are a multitude of graphic organizers available, with many formats being flexible enough for a variety of content areas. Below I will highlight some different graphic organizer formats that my PSTs have found useful and discuss how I utilized them in my courses. Within each of these formats, there are opportunities for me, as the instructor, to adjust the amount of scaffolding and support I provide.

Matrix Chart

A matrix chart (Table 12) is useful for comparing two or more concepts and is an alternative to the Venn diagram. Unlike a Venn diagram, which focuses on overlapping similarities and differences in a more open-ended format, the matrix chart format allows the instructor to specify specific areas for comparison if needed. This targeted approach helps emphasize the most relevant aspects of the material, ensuring that students focus on critical connections rather than becoming overwhelmed by extraneous details. The matrix format also encourages clarity and precision in comparison, making it especially valuable when dealing with complex concepts that require a more focused analysis.

I utilize this format for PSTs who indicate a preference or need for structured note-taking, as it provides a clear visual framework for organizing information. Depending on the needs of the PST, I may provide the format with predetermined categories for comparison, such as characteristics, examples, and applications, or leave it blank for students to determine relevant points on their own. For example, when comparing instructional strategies like direct instruction, inquiry-based learning, and cooperative learning, the matrix chart might include columns for aspects such as student engagement level, teacher role, and assessment methods.

This approach not only supports PSTs who benefit from structured guidance but also fosters critical thinking by encouraging them to analyze and categorize information in a meaningful way. Additionally, matrix charts can serve as useful study tools, helping PSTs review and synthesize key concepts efficiently.

Table 12 Matrix Chart Example

Directions: Using information from today's class discussion and course readings, complete the following chart comparing and contrasting different learning theories using the characteristics in the far-left column.

Characteristic	Behaviorism	Cognitivism	Constructivism
Teacher's role			
Students' role			
Focus of the learning			
Key instructional strategies			
Assessment practices			
Classroom environment			
Cultural relevance			
Limitations			

Inquiry Chart

The inquiry chart (Table 13; Stanley, 2022) is a type of graphic organizer that pushes students to go beyond the information learned in class to create their own questions on a topic and conduct brief research to answer these questions and synthesize what they learn from multiple sources. PSTs in my courses have utilized these charts to gain a deeper understanding of topics ranging from supporting emergent readers who are nonnative speakers of English to how schools and districts use the Danielson Framework as a tool for teacher evaluation and/or teacher professional development. For PSTs who need additional support, I may provide one pre-created question to get them started or provide some question stems (examples below) to support them in creating their own questions. Once the charts are completed, I typically provide an opportunity for PSTs to share what they learned, either through small-group discussions (in larger classes) or whole-class discussion (when I have a small number of students). I have also engaged PSTs in creating a shared document to which they contribute what they learned in their research.

Sample Question Stems

- In what ways does research support or challenge common assumptions about… ?

Table 13 Inquiry Chart Example

Directions: For the topic assigned, develop three specific questions to which you hope to find answers. Find answers to your questions using a minimum of three reputable sources. Feel free to put additional notes that may be helpful in the final column. After collecting information from each of your resources, synthesize the information you found in response to each of your questions.

	Topic:			
	Question 1	**Question 2**	**Question 3**	**Additional Notes or Questions**
Text 1				
Text 2				
Text 3				
Synthesis				

- What are the key challenges associated with… ?
- How does… impact student outcomes?
- What strategies have been found effective in… ?
- How does research define best practices for… ?
- What are the potential benefits and drawbacks of… ?
- How does [topic] compare across different educational settings or populations?
- What might [topic] look like in my clinical placement context?
- What historical or contextual factors have shaped current practices in… ?
- What challenges do educators face when implementing… ?
- How has our understanding of [topic] evolved over time?
- How does [topic] align with or challenge current educational standards and policies?

Technology Tools

There are a wide variety of technology tools commonly available to support students as they engage with content. In particular, text-to-speech and speech-to-text provide scaffolding for students and are now available on most devices. These tools are invaluable for fostering inclusivity, as they support diverse learning needs and can reduce barriers to accessing information.

Text-to-speech allows students to listen to written material, making almost any text into an audiobook. For PSTs who may not be fast readers due to neurodiversity or other differences, this can be a powerful support as the texts they engage with become increasingly complex. Speech-to-text, which simply puts the spoken word into a written format, is a tool I recommend to PSTs who struggle to get their thoughts into writing. The freedom to simply talk through their ideas and have them appear on the screen as a starting point often breaks through the initial writer's block. For many, it also removes their own stress about grammar and mechanics in that first draft since the computer will be taking care of many of those elements initially. This can significantly boost confidence, especially for students who might feel anxious about the quality of their writing, as it frees them to focus more on content development and less on surface-level errors.

Reflection and Discussion Questions

"As a Teacher Educator" reflection questions are for the course instructor to reflect on their utilization of DI. "As a Learner" and "As an Educator" questions are for PSTs to reflect on their experience with differentiation as a learner and how they can apply that experience to their future classrooms. The two sets of questions consider the dual roles of PSTs in the teacher educator program. It is recommended that PSTs have an opportunity to reflect on these questions individually before sharing and discussing them with peers.

As a Teacher Educator:

1 Can you identify specific examples where differentiation by content and by process overlap in your teaching? How do you address this overlap to enhance clarity and effectiveness?

2 How do you currently differentiate the way PSTs engage with and make sense of course materials? What strategies have you found most effective, and why?

3 How do you determine when scaffolding is necessary for PSTs? What types of scaffolding strategies (e.g., graphic organizers, sentence stems, step-by-step checklists) could you incorporate into your lessons to support their success?

4 What scaffolding techniques do you find most effective in supporting students who need additional practice?

5. How do you provide additional challenge for advanced learners without it feeling inequitable or like busy work?
6. How do you currently structure directions for complex tasks to avoid cognitive overload?
7. How do you introduce essential vocabulary or concepts before a lesson?
8. How often do you provide models of tasks for students, and in what ways do you explain the reasoning behind these models? How do students respond to this approach?
9. What criteria do you use to create flexible groups for activities? How do you balance group composition to foster collaboration and accountability?
10. How do you measure the effectiveness of differentiated process strategies in terms of student engagement and understanding? What feedback mechanisms do you use?
11. What are some challenges you've encountered when implementing differentiation by process, and how have you addressed them?

As a Learner:

1. Think about a time in this or another class when you felt overwhelmed by instructions or a task. How did breaking down steps into smaller parts (or the lack thereof) impact your ability to succeed?
2. Reflecting on your own learning experience, how have you benefited from engaging with course materials in multiple formats (e.g., reading, listening, watching videos)? How do these different modalities support your understanding of the content?
3. How have you experienced scaffolding strategies (e.g., graphic organizers, step-by-step guides, sentence stems) in your coursework? In what ways did these supports help you organize or process information?
4. Reflect on an activity that involved collaboration or group work (e.g., jigsaw, gallery walk). What did you learn from your peers during this activity that you may not have learned independently?
5. Reflect on how the use of technology has influenced your ability to manage tasks, organize your thoughts, or engage with course content. Are there any tools that you found particularly helpful?

6 What supports or adjustments have you found helpful for your learning, and how can you communicate these needs to instructors or colleagues in the future?

7 What specific differentiation strategies have you noticed your instructor using in this class? How do these strategies impact your engagement and success?

As an Educator:

1 How might you use strategies like breaking down steps, modeling tasks, or flexible grouping in your own classroom? How would you adapt them to different grade levels or subject areas?

2 When designing lessons or activities, how will you determine whether a task is appropriately challenging for your students? How can you adjust complexity for learners at different levels?

3 During discussions or group activities, what teaching methods did your peers use that you found particularly effective? How could you adapt these methods for your future classroom?

4 Reflect on the jigsaw strategy or other collaborative activities you've experienced. How would you implement these in your classroom to ensure accountability and engagement from all students?

5 How will you ensure that differentiation by process supports equitable learning opportunities for all students, including those who may need more time or additional practice?

6 How does your instructor model complex tasks or expectations? How could you replicate this practice in your teaching?

6 Differentiation by Product

Differentiating instruction by product is defined as varying the ways in which students demonstrate their growth and proficiency. Although many see this level of differentiation as simply providing students with choice in how they present their learning, effective product differentiation requires thoughtful planning on the part of the teacher. Differentiating by product should include opportunities for students to show their knowledge in a variety of ways while balancing the demands (cognitive, time, resources) of each option so the student experience is equitable regardless of the product choice. Differentiating by product may also include levels of scaffolding appropriate to the differing needs of students, such as the Major Assignment Tasks Checklist (see Chapter 5). Finally, differentiating by product can include a variety of options regarding the format in which students share their knowledge and skill, ranging from traditional written products to performative and interpersonal tasks (Table 14), while also requiring students to demonstrate the same depth of knowledge regardless of product format.

When preparing for product differentiation, as with any assessment, it is vital to consider the standards and student learning outcomes for the course, unit, or lesson. (For more on planning with purposeful application of the standards and student outcomes in mind, read up on Universal Design for Learning at https://udlguidelines.cast.org.) In the examples that follow, you will note purposeful parallels among the various choices provided. In one example choice project (Table 16), two options are given that align with each task objective. The objectives listed are learning outcomes for the course that I designed the menu project to address. In the menu example below (Table 19), the tasks for each level (appetizer, main dish, side dish) are created to require approximately the same amount of effort at the same level of Bloom's taxonomy across the tasks.

Table 14 Possible Product Modalities for Differentiated Products

Written (communication using traditional text with little emphasis on multimodal elements)	<ul><li>Quiz or exam (multiple-choice and/or open-ended prompts)</li><li>Lesson or unit plan</li><li>Essay/report<ul><li>Summary of material</li><li>Research report</li><li>Literature review</li><li>Case study (analysis or creation)</li><li>Position paper</li><li>White paper</li><li>Policy analysis</li><li>Action plan for addressing a concern</li><li>Editorial or advocacy letter</li><li>Analysis/critique of a resource</li></ul></li><li>Journal entries<ul><li>Reflection on classroom experiences</li><li>From the perspective of an individual in a different role (parent, student, principal, etc.)</li></ul></li><li>Field notes</li><li>Glossary of relevant terminology</li><li>Annotated bibliography</li><li>Newspaper or newsletter article</li><li>Memo or other internal school communication</li><li>Letter</li><li>Poem</li><li>Create a test or other assessment with answer key</li><li>Graphic organizer (utilize or create)</li><li>Handbook or user's guide</li><li>Grant proposal</li></ul>
Multimodal (includes a mix of text and visuals, as well as opportunities for other modalities utilized to support communication)	<ul><li>Poster</li><li>Brochure</li><li>Blog post</li><li>Wiki post</li><li>Slideshow presentation (PowerPoint, Google Slides, Prezi, etc.)</li><li>Diagram, map, model, graph, or flowchart</li><li>Storyboard</li><li>Infographic</li><li>Anchor chart</li></ul>

	- Web page/website
	  - Informational
	  - Tutorial
	  - Interactive learning module
	  - Digital magazine
	- Escape room activity
	- Online book
	- Comic strip
	- Advertisement (billboard, social media, other targeted medium)
	- ABC book (e.g., the ABCs of assessment)
	- Board game
	- App
	- Annotated playlist (songs, videos, podcasts that relate to a specific theme)
	- Photo essay or visual story (digital storytelling)
	- Traditional art forms

Performative
(provides opportunities for the product to be shared in a way that is impacted by the presenter's speaking skill or presentation choices in a one-way sharing of knowledge)
	- Podcast
	- Video (can be traditional recording, animation, stop-motion, etc.)
	  - Tutorial
	  - Documentary
	  - Analysis of a case or situation
	  - Newscast
	  - Commercial
	  - Public service announcement
	  - Lesson demonstration in a clinical placement
	- Speech or other oral presentation (e.g., demonstration)
	- Oral storytelling

Interpersonal (provides opportunities for active engagement with the presenter's audience)	- Interview an expert - Conduct a mock interview - Role-play or simulation of interactions - Participate in a debate or mock trial - Hold a panel discussion on the topic - Lead a workshop - Teach a sample lesson to peers - Facilitate a whole-class discussion - Engage in a one-on-one discussion with the instructor

Notes: 1. Some products may not fit cleanly into a single modality. In such cases, I have placed the product into a single modality for clarity. 2. Some of the ideas in the written category could easily be shifted to other modalities. For example, a research report could be presented as a podcast or video.

Another aspect of product differentiation to consider is how many options to offer. Too many choices may result in "choice overload" and lead to students feeling overwhelmed or regretting the option selected (Beymer & Thompson, 2015). With this in mind, I typically start with two to three options for each task objective (Table 16) or category (Tables 17 and 20) within a menu project or other product differentiation assignment.

I have utilized a variety of differentiated products within my own courses, which have been met with positive responses from the preservice teachers (PSTs) in my courses from the moment they are introduced, as evidenced by the student feedback below:

> *Overall I am really excited for this class and am really curious about the 100 point projects with the fact that we can choose what we want to do, I love that! —Student in K–8 language arts methods course, fall 2020*

General Strategies

Additional Check-Ins for PSTs Who Need More Structure

Differentiating by product means providing PSTs multiple ways to demonstrate their learning. However, as previously mentioned, some PSTs may need additional structure when engaging in open-ended and multiple-choice assignments. For those who need additional structure, frequent check-ins can guide them toward successful completion of differentiated products. Strategies include the following:

- Scaffolded product expectations: Break projects into smaller components with checkpoints to ensure that students are progressing toward their final product. This can be done through an assignment checklist (see Chapter 5, Figure 13) or other tools. This type of tool will provide PSTs with concrete ways to self-monitor their progress.
- Scheduled one-on-one meetings: One-on-one meetings with the instructor can provide support by reviewing progress, making and reflecting on short-term goals, and clarifying areas of confusion. These meetings can also provide immediate and actionable feedback and build PSTs' confidence in moving forward with the project. If one-on-one meetings are not possible due to class size or other constraints,

PSTs can meet in small peer groups to discuss prompts and identify questions to ask the instructor in a whole-class debrief. The meeting can be guided by prompts similar to the following, with all prompts appropriate for one-on-one meetings and small-group meetings:
- Can you walk me through where you are in your project right now?
- Which tasks from the choices did you choose? Why did you select those options?
- What aspects of your project are going well so far?
- How do you feel about the quality of your work on this project so far? Are there areas you would like to improve?
- Are there areas in which you need additional guidance or resources?
- What type of feedback would be most helpful right now?
- What are your next steps for completing your project?

Student Goal Setting and Product Differentiation

In a differentiated classroom, PSTs should have the opportunity to set personal learning goals related to the products they create. This ensures that assessment is about not only what students learn but also how they choose to express their understanding. This can be approached through any of the following strategies:

- Product selection based on goals: Allow PSTs to choose how they will demonstrate mastery—through an essay, video, artistic representation, podcast, or another medium that aligns with and/or supports their personal goals for growth and development. For example, a PST who is confident in their ability to create traditional written projects may choose to complete a task in a multimodal format, such as an infographic, to engage with educational technology tools they hope to utilize in their future classroom within a safe and structured environment to meet a personal goal for professional growth in utilization of education technology.

- Reflection and self-assessment: Encouraging PSTs to evaluate how well their chosen product met their learning goals and what they would improve is a natural next step. This can be an opportunity to reflect in a written format, through discussions with peers, or in one-on-one meetings with the course instructor. The prompts below can be utilized for any of the three reflection formats previously mentioned:

- How effectively does your finished product reflect the course learning outcome identified for the task?
- What connections can you make between your finished product or the process of creating it and your future teaching practice/classroom?
- Why did you choose this format to share your learning? Was it an effective choice for sharing your learning *and* for working toward your personal learning goals?
- If you had more time or resources, are there any changes you would make to your final product?
- What skills or knowledge do you want to develop further in future projects?

By linking goal setting to differentiated products, students take ownership of both their learning process and how they showcase their knowledge.

Opportunities to Integrate PSTs' Culture Through Product Differentiation

A powerful way to differentiate through product is to provide opportunities for PSTs to integrate their cultural backgrounds into their projects. This makes learning more meaningful and personally relevant. Strategies for this include the following:

- Culturally relevant product choices: Encourage PSTs to express their understanding through culturally significant formats, such as oral storytelling, music, or traditional art forms, which provides opportunities for PSTs to integrate their cultural backgrounds into their learning. Examples are the following:
  - For a task focusing on analysis of historical events, PSTs could research events from their own culture whose narratives parallel or counter those studied in class and present their findings through role-play, storytelling, or traditional art.
  - If PSTs are creating lesson plans to support elementary students in mathematics concepts such as geometry and geometric patterns or STEM content such as engineering principles, provide opportunities for the PSTs to integrate examples from their own cultures within the plans.
- Flexible final product formats: Provide PSTs with opportunities to choose how they demonstrate learning based on their personal

experiences—such as writing a narrative from the perspective of a historical figure or current leader in their culture or creating a multimedia presentation that ties the topic to their cultural background. Another example is for PSTs to interview members of their family and/or community regarding course topics and how they are or can be tied to elements of their culture or traditional knowledge. This information could be shared through a podcast, video, traditional art form, or oral storytelling. This can also increase the relevance of material to PSTs lives, experiences, and future teaching.
- Authentic audience opportunities: Provide options for PSTs to share their products with their families, community members, or peers, including those who relate to their cultural perspectives. This can include collaborations with organizations such as local cultural groups, heritage organizations, community centers, or museums.

Specific Strategies and Tools

RAFT (Role, Audience, Format, Topic) Response

RAFT writing prompts can be utilized to allow PSTs to consider content from different perspectives and for a variety of purposes. In this format, the PST chooses or is assigned a role (e.g., teacher, student, parent, administrator), target audience (e.g., colleague, parent group), format of the communication (e.g., professional development presentation, e-mail, memo), and the specific topic of the communication (e.g., student assessment scores, classroom management concern, upcoming field trip). I often use this format in conjunction with case studies or after introducing new concepts to get PSTs thinking about the real-world applications of the material. This may mean assigning some aspects of the assignment, such as the topic or role, while leaving the remaining elements up to the PST.

Example RAFT prompts are the following:

- After reading the case study in this module, choose one of the individuals in the case and create a RAFT in which they communicate their perception of the situation and present some possible solutions to another individual in the scenario.
- Using information you learned in this module about classroom management, create a RAFT that is a communication from a teacher

at a grade level of your choice to parents of the students in the class letting them know classroom norms and expectations. You may select the format in which to communicate this information.
- Reflect on a recent classroom experience from practicum this semester using the RAFT format. You can choose your audience (e.g., fellow teachers, students, parents) and format (e.g., letter, report, video) to communicate your reflection. Choose the specific experience you want to reflect on, such as a lesson that went well or a challenge you faced.
- In a RAFT format, take on a role you think is relevant (e.g., teacher, tutor, parent) and create a product (e.g., pamphlet, e-mail, infographic) that offers advice to parents on how they can support their child's literacy and numeracy learning at home.
- Using the RAFT format, create an outline for a professional development workshop for teachers in a grade level/content area of your choice using main points from today's readings and discussion. You may consider what points would be most important from the perspective of a teacher colleague, administrator, or other role within the school community.

The example RAFT Response Rubric (Table 15) provides a structured yet flexible framework for assessing student work in a way that prioritizes critical thinking, content accuracy, and audience awareness while allowing for differentiation of any element within the RAFT as well as allowing for the RAFT to be completed in a variety of formats. This single-point rubric is designed to help PSTs focus on meeting expectations while also providing space for targeted feedback on areas for growth and excellence. (This rubric format will be discussed in more detail later in this chapter.) By maintaining consistent expectations across all RAFT responses—regardless of the chosen role, audience, format, or topic—the rubric ensures that each response is assessed based on their ability to demonstrate depth of understanding, application of course concepts, and effective communication.

When using this rubric, I would highlight or otherwise identify where the submission is (below target, target, or above target) for each area (e.g., role and perspective, audience awareness) and provide specific feedback in the last column regarding why the submission met/did not meet/exceeded target. Feedback for the last of the example prompts using this rubric could be worded like this for meeting the target in the role and perspective category:

You effectively take on the role of a teacher colleague, demonstrating an understanding of professional development needs. Your perspective is appropriate for the context. To move to "above target," consider incorporating realistic concerns or experiences that teachers in your chosen grade level/content area might have. For example, if discussing classroom management strategies, you could highlight common struggles teachers face, such as managing transitions or engaging reluctant learners.

Table 15 Example Rubric for RAFT Response

Above Target: Evidence of Exceeding Standards	Target: Expectations for RAFT Response	Below Target: Areas That Need Improvement	Specific Feedback
Role and perspective: PST goes beyond expectations, providing deep insight, nuance, or particularly strong voice and perspective in the response.	Role and perspective: PST maintains a clear and authentic role, demonstrating a well-developed understanding of the assigned or chosen perspective.	Role and perspective: PST does not clearly maintain the assigned or chosen role, or the perspective lacks depth and authenticity.	
Audience awareness: PST skillfully adapts the message with exceptional awareness of the audience, demonstrating a sophisticated understanding of communication.	Audience awareness: PST effectively tailors the message to the audience, using appropriate tone, language, and details.	Audience awareness: Message is not well tailored to the intended audience; tone, language, or details may be inappropriate or inconsistent.	
Format and structure: PST creatively and strategically uses the format to enhance communication, making the response particularly engaging or effective.	Format and structure: PST effectively utilizes the chosen format, ensuring clarity, organization, and adherence to appropriate conventions.	Format and structure: Chosen format is unclear, inconsistent, or ineffective in conveying the message.	

Above Target: Evidence of Exceeding Standards	Target: Expectations for RAFT Response	Below Target: Areas That Need Improvement	Specific Feedback
Content and accuracy: PST provides exceptional depth, using rich details, strong supporting evidence, or an insightful perspective on the topic.	Content and accuracy: PST demonstrates strong understanding of the topic with accurate, relevant, and well-supported ideas.	Content and accuracy: Ideas are underdeveloped, inaccurate, or lacking relevance to the topic.	
Application and critical thinking: PST makes highly relevant and insightful connections, demonstrating exceptional critical thinking and application.	Application and critical thinking: PST thoughtfully applies concepts to a real-world context, offering insightful analysis and connections.	PST makes limited or surface-level connections, with minimal evidence of critical thinking or meaningful application. Analysis may be general, incomplete, or lack clear connection to concepts or real-world contexts.	
Mechanics and clarity: PST's writing or presentation is exceptionally well crafted, demonstrating a high level of professionalism, clarity, and refinement.	Mechanics and clarity: PST's writing or presentation is clear, polished, and free of distracting errors.	Mechanics and clarity: PST's writing or presentation lacks clarity or contains multiple mechanical or grammatical errors that distract from the message. Organization or phrasing may impede understanding or reflect limited attention to professional communication standards.	

Choice Boards

Choice boards (also called menu assignments) are a flexible tool for assessing student understanding or application of content and skills. These assignments provide multiple project options for students to choose from. Options should provide opportunities for students to utilize a variety of tools and formats to demonstrate their learning. When creating the menu project, be explicit about the objective of each set of tasks so that students understand what knowledge or skills they are expected to demonstrate in completing the task.

Below are examples of three different formats that can be used for choice boards. The first is a shortened example of a points project. I often do a 100 points project within my English language arts (ELA) methods course, but in compacted semesters I have reduced it to a lower point value (typically 50 points). This project requires PSTs to select from a range of projects with assigned points based on the complexity of each task, with a goal of reaching the expected final value. In this example menu project (Table 16), the first learning objective is for PSTs to demonstrate their understanding and application of literacy instructional practices, while the second requires PSTs to analyze and critique teacher resources. For each objective, students have multiple task options, each of which requires students to utilize different modes of presentation and to engage with varying source materials. Each task includes a clear rationale (why am I doing this?) and connection to course learning outcomes. All tasks utilize a common rubric for assessment (Table 17). I offer scaffolded due dates for this assignment, with the first due date requiring 20 points worth of tasks completed if the full project is for 100 points. Based on the feedback they receive on their first submission, PSTs can then move forward confident in their understanding of the expectations and application of the project rubric (Table 17). I also allow PSTs to complete as many tasks as they need to earn the full number of points. Thus, if a PST's first submission is a 20-point task that earns them only 15 points, they can do an additional task or simply choose a task with a higher point value to make up the points they did not earn in that initial task.

The rubric for this task is an analytic rubric divided into six sections, with each section assigned between 10 and 25 percent of the task assessment score. Each section provides opportunities for specific growth feedback to support PSTs as they engage in their next task choice. For example, a PST who earns a three out of four in the completeness section could be provided the following feedback: "In future tasks, be sure to revisit the task guidelines to double-check that you have included all required elements. The inclusion of detailed directions for this station activity would have strengthened this submission."

The second example (Table 18) is a menu that uses a tic-tac-toe format. Like other formats in this chapter, the tic-tac-toe format provides student choice within a structure that ensures that PSTs have an opportunity to demonstrate

Table 16 Example 100-Point Project Excerpt

Task Objective (choose one activity for each objective)	Activity Options	Rationale and Relevant Course Objective
Demonstrate understanding and application of literacy instructional practices	Station activity (20 points)—Create a single-station activity that can be utilized to support students in building their skills in one area of literacy. It can be individual or collaborative. The station activity should take the average student approximately 10 minutes to complete. Include the following information: * Standard(s) met by the station * Materials and teacher prep needed * Full directions for the station * Student-friendly directions for the station * A description of the finished student product from the station * One or two paragraphs explaining how this station supports student growth in this specific area of literacy Support your statements with citations from reliable sources.	The goal of this activity is to provide you with an opportunity to create a station activity that can be used in your field placement and/or your future classroom to support student literacy growth. Course objectives: 3—Gain an understanding and appreciation of the theories and principles for teaching ELA in the classroom. 5—Apply and analyze various strategies to enhance reading, writing, speaking, media usage, and other forms of literacy across disciplines.

Lesson modification (20 points)—Select a preexisting online lesson from any content area outside reading/language arts (social studies, science, mathematics, physical education, etc.) Look through the lesson plan as it is and consider what literacy element could be added to/improve this lesson. Could it be improved by the addition of an explicit vocabulary activity? Are some higher-order questions needed to push students beyond basic comprehension of material? Create a new literacy-based component for this lesson resource. Include clear teacher and student directions that would allow anyone to pick up the lesson and seamlessly weave this new component into the existing resource. This may include creating student examples, writing possible answers to questions posed, and so on. Include information supporting your addition to the lesson as an activity that boosts student literacy growth, with appropriate citations. Make sure you also include a full citation for the lesson resource your component is written to accompany.	The goal of this assignment is to provide you with an opportunity to think critically about an existing resource and use your knowledge of best practices to add to/improve the lesson. Course objectives: 1—Develop meaningful, integrated, responsive, rigorous, developmentally appropriate, and active ELA learning experiences for K–8 students of varying abilities, age levels, and exceptionalities across disciplines. 5—Apply and analyze various strategies to enhance reading, writing, speaking, media usage, and other forms of literacy across disciplines.

Task Objective (choose one activity for each objective)	Activity Options	Rationale and Relevant Course Objective
Analyze and critique available resources for teachers	Annotated resource list (20 points)—Create an annotated list of online resources for educators focused on one specific area of literacy (comprehension, phonics, vocabulary, grammar, etc.). This list should contain at least 10 resources (full APA citation and an annotation describing and assessing the value of the source). Sources can include specific lesson ideas, student activities and games, or articles to support teachers in developing students' skills in this area. Do not include the same website for more than two resources. For example, do not include eight activities from ReadWriteThink.org. Be sure all the resources you list are free for teacher and student use. No pay subscription sites! You can present this annotated list in any format you wish. Some options include a blog post, PowerPoint, or infographic.	The goal of this activity is to provide you with the opportunity to explore and critique some of the many online resources available for literacy teachers. Course objectives: 1—Develop meaningful, integrated, responsive, rigorous, developmentally appropriate, and active ELA learning experiences for K–8 students of varying abilities, age levels, and exceptionalities across disciplines. 3—Gain an understanding and appreciation of the theories and principles for teaching ELA in the classroom. 5—Apply and analyze various strategies to enhance reading, writing, speaking, media usage, and other forms of literacy across disciplines.
	Professional book critique (30 points)—Select a literacy-focused professional book for teachers (defined as a book that provides teachers with pedagogical knowledge and instructional strategies as opposed to specific	The goal of this assignment is to provide you with an opportunity to think critically about an existing professional resource and use your knowledge of best practices to consider the strengths and weaknesses of the resource.

	Course objectives:3—Gain an understanding and appreciation of the theories and principles for teaching ELA in the classroom. 5—Apply and analyze various strategies to enhance reading, writing, speaking, media usage, and other forms of literacy across disciplines.
lesson ideas). This *cannot* be a book you have read/bought for another course. Read the book and create a review/critique of this resource. Your review/critique should include a full citation for the text and address the following: * Information about the author(s) or editor(s): What are their credentials? What makes them experts? Go beyond the book blurb! Cite sources outside the book that talk about the author's credentials. * Background knowledge needed by the reader. (What terminology does the reader need to know, for example?) * Organization of the book: Is it logical? Is the layout clear and appealing? Are there sidebars to highlight important or interesting points? * Visuals: Are there charts, tables, or examples of student work included? What do these add? If visuals are included, are they helpful and meaningful? * Strategies included: Are there a variety of strategies included? Does the book provide enough information to support the reader in implementing the pedagogical strategies shared? * Are additional resources (resources outside the text, such as additional	

Task Objective (choose one activity for each objective)	Activity Options	Rationale and Relevant Course Objective
	books, websites, etc.) suggested for further reading? If so, are they valuable? Explain. * Is research utilized, both through in-text citations and an end references list, to support the information and ideas being shared? * Give two to three big takeaways from the book. * Are there any ideas in the book you are unsure about, disagree with, or feel need further clarification? * What do you feel is one strength of this book? * What do you feel is one weakness of this book? Make sure to cite sources in your critique as appropriate. This may include information on gradual release of responsibility, Bloom's taxonomy, and instructional practices discussed within the text.	

Table 17 Example Rubric: 100-Point Project Analytic Rubric

Each task completed will be graded utilizing the following rubric. The score on the rubric will then be used to determine how many of the possible points you receive for that task. You will notice that inclusion of citations is not included in the rubric; that is because lack of citations will constitute plagiarism, resulting in zero points for that task.

Description	4	3	2	1
Completeness (10%)	The task contains all the required aspects of the assignment.	The task is missing one component of the assignment.	The task is missing no more than two components of the assignment.	The task does not meet the requirements of the assignment (more than two components missing).
Organization and presentation (15%)	The task is well organized, with a clear structure and logical flow. Information is presented in an easily digestible format, using appropriate headings and a professional tone throughout.	The task is organized but may have minor issues with flow or clarity. Some sections could be better structured for easier readability.	The task lacks clear structure or is difficult to follow in places. Information is presented in a scattered or unclear manner, making it harder to understand.	The task is poorly organized, lacking logical flow. Sections are jumbled, making it difficult to follow the content or objectives.
Correctness of citations (15%)	Citations are correctly included within the project, including internal citations and a reference page.	An attempt at correctly citing sources is included, including internal citations and a reference page.	An attempt at correctly citing sources is included, including one of the following: internal citations or a reference page.	An attempt at citing sources is included but is rudimentary and shows little to no understanding of APA citation format.

Description	4	3	2	1
Content knowledge (25%)	The task demonstrates comprehensive and sophisticated knowledge of literacy best practices. Information is accurate and detailed and reflects a deep understanding of literacy concepts.	The task demonstrates a solid understanding of literacy best practices. Information is mostly accurate and reflects a good understanding of literacy concepts, though some areas may lack depth.	The task demonstrates basic understanding of literacy best practices, relying primarily on class materials. Some concepts may be inaccurate or underdeveloped.	The task demonstrates limited or superficial understanding of literacy best practices. The content lacks accuracy and depth, with unclear or missing connections to foundational literacy concepts.
Application of literacy strategies (25%)	The PST effectively applies literacy strategies relevant to the course objective(s) related to the task in a clear and meaningful way that is highly relevant to the task. The application is innovative, demonstrating thoughtful adaptation of strategies to support student learning.	The PST applies literacy strategies in a way that is relevant to the course objective(s) related to the task, with some appropriate adaptation. The strategies are appropriate for the task and context but may not be fully developed or detailed.	The PST applies literacy strategies in a way that is somewhat relevant to the course objective(s) related to the task but lacks depth or specificity in how they would be implemented in the classroom. Some strategies may not be fully connected to the objectives.	The PST struggles to apply literacy strategies in a way that is relevant to the course objective(s) related to the task. The strategies are vague, underdeveloped, or not aligned with the task's objectives.

| Use of research and sources (10%) | The PST incorporates three or more high-quality, reliable sources outside course readings that directly support and enhance the content. The sources are carefully selected and well integrated and strengthen the overall argument of the task. | The PST includes one or two relevant sources outside course readings that support the content. The sources are appropriate but could be more varied or more deeply connected to the literacy practices being discussed. | The PST uses one or two sources outside course readings, but they are not clearly relevant or do not significantly support the content. There is a limited use of outside research to back up claims. | The PST uses no outside sources and/or the sources that are used are less relevant or do not adequately support the assignment's claims. |

Grading examples:
Suppose that you did a 10-point task. Your score for each section is 4, 3, 4, 3, 3. Thus, for organization and presentation, in which you earned a 3 out of 4, you would multiply ¾ times 15%, which is 11.25%. After calculating all percentages, you would earn 83.75% of the points possible. Thus, you would get 8.38 of the possible 10 points for the task.

Table 18 Tic-Tac-Toe Example

Course objective addressed: PSTs will be able to unpack relevant content area standards and utilize them to plan instruction for students in grades K–8. Directions: For each of the three levels of the revised Bloom's taxonomy (Understand, Apply, Evaluate), choose one activity. Your choices should make a straight line (horizontal, vertical of diagonal) like a winning tic-tac-toe board. Unless otherwise noted, your response can be in a written format of your choice (traditional written product, presentation, infographic, etc.) or in an audiovisual format (video, podcast, etc.) appropriate to sharing the relevant information.

Understand	Create a chart with four columns: Standard, key skills or actions (verbs), content focus (nouns), and student outcome/goal. Complete the chart with three content area standards from a grade level of your choice. Create a student outcome/learning objective to align with each standard.	Select a content area strand (e.g., operations and algebraic thinking) for a single grade level. Select at least four standards from the chosen strand and do the following for each standard: 1. Highlight key verbs (e.g., analyze, solve) and nouns (e.g., equations, fractions). 2. Based on the highlighted words, explain in your own words what students should know and be able to do to show proficiency in that standard.	Imagine you are planning three lessons (one on each of the following): **a** Counting by 10s to 100 (kindergarten) **b** Adding four-digit numbers (grade 2) **c** Solving multistep word problems that include decimals or fractions (grade 7) Identify the most relevant standard for the lesson. For each standard, identify the key verbs (e.g., analyze, solve) and nouns (e.g., equations, fractions). Using this information, write a student outcome/learning objective for each lesson.

Apply	Select one content area standard for a grade of your choice. (It can be a standard you used in another activity on the board.) Using this standard, do the following: 1. Determine what prerequisite knowledge students need to begin working toward proficiency in this standard. 2. Determine potential challenges or misconceptions students may have as they engage in this standard. 3. Using course resources, create an instructional activity addressing the selected standard. It may be an activity for whole-group instruction or small-group/individual practice.	Interview an experienced K8 teacher about how they use content area standards in their lesson planning. Some suggested questions are the following: 1. How do you unpack standards when planning instruction? 2. How do you prioritize standards when planning instruction? 3. Can you give an example of a recent lesson and the standard it addressed? 4. What challenges have you faced when aligning lessons with standards? After the interview, write up a reflection on what you learned and how you can apply it to your lesson planning. What are the big takeaways? What tips or ideas will stick with you?	Select a specific content area standard and create a student-friendly anchor chart for use in the classroom. The anchor chart should include the following: 1. The language of the standard in student-friendly terms (consider an "I can…" statement). 2. Examples or visuals to demonstrate the concept 3. Key vocabulary students should know related to the standard 4. Tips or steps for success

Evaluate	Select one of the sample lessons plans in this week's module and evaluate its alignment with the identified standard. 1. Evaluate the alignment of the stated learning outcomes to the standard. 2. Identify where and how the standard is addressed in the lesson plan. 3. Assess the activities and assessments within the lesson plan. Are they sufficient to meet the stated standard? 4. Recommend adjustments, additions, or adaptations to the lesson to better meet the stated standard.	Select one of the student work samples in this week's module and evaluate using the following guiding questions: 1. Does this work demonstrate mastery of the stated standard? 2. What specific criteria within the standard is met or unmet? Use examples from the student work sample to support your analysis. 3. What are some instructional adjustments or specific instructional strategies that could be used to support students who have not yet reached proficiency in this standard?	Select one of the sample assessments in this week's module and evaluate its alignment with the identified standard. 1. Does the assessment effectively measure the skills and/or knowledge in the selected standard? Use evidence from the standard and the assessment to support your response. 2. Identify any areas in which the assessment does not align with the selected standard. 3. Propose specific revisions or an alternative method of assessment that might better address the standard.

the knowledge or skills necessary to demonstrate growth or proficiency in the stated standard(s) or objective(s). Table 18 focuses on a single learning objective and provides task options at three different levels of complexity using the revised version of Bloom's taxonomy (Anderson & Krathwohl, 2001). This format could also be used to address three different standards or objectives, with one row of the board dedicated to each. For this example, I utilized a single-point rubric (Table 19). This rubric format is more open-ended and provides an opportunity for specific feedback on what is missing in terms of meeting the expectations or on the ways in which the task exceeds the expectations. I have adapted the format to include a column in which I can include feedback regarding how the task met the stated expectations if applicable. While this type of rubric often takes less time to create, it may take more time to complete due to its open-ended nature. However, PSTs' responses to this rubric format in my courses have been very positive, particularly due to the level of feedback provided and the opportunity this rubric format provides for self-reflection due to its simplicity (Fluckiger, 2010).

For this second example choice board, below-target feedback for the first task in the "Apply" level might look like this: "In your activity design, it's clear you've chosen a relevant standard, but your explanation of prerequisite knowledge and potential misconceptions could use more detail. You've selected an instructional activity, but you need to provide more specific connections between the activity and the challenges students may face." Feedback for a submission that meets the target might state,

> *You've chosen a good standard and clearly identified the prerequisite knowledge and potential student misconceptions. The instructional activity you created is well aligned to the selected standard and considers how to support students who lack the prerequisite knowledge or who have some of the stated misconceptions. Consider challenging yourself by expanding on how you plan to differentiate the activity or support students who might struggle. Including specific strategies to address potential misconceptions or gaps would make the activity even stronger.*

Finally, feedback for a submission that is assessed as "Above Target" might state,

> *Your application of pedagogy and content knowledge is thorough. You've not only identified relevant standards and misconceptions but also thoughtfully designed an instructional activity with multiple strategies for addressing*

Table 19 Single-Point Rubric for Tic-Tac-Toe Activity

Course objective addressed: PSTs will be able to unpack relevant content area standards and utilize them to plan instruction for students in grades K–8.

Below Target Areas That Need Improvement	Target (expectations for this row of tasks)	At Target: Evidence of Meeting Standards	Above Target Evidence of Exceeding Standards
	Understand: PST demonstrates the ability to identify key skills and knowledge within content area standards and communicate in their own words what proficiency for this standard looks like.		
	Apply: PST demonstrates the ability to apply their knowledge and learning of pedagogy and content area standards to their own creation of lesson plans and/or resources.		
	Evaluate: PST demonstrates the ability to utilize standards to guide their evaluation of resources or student work, including identification of gaps in alignment and recommendations for adjustments to better support student success in meeting proficiency in the identified standard.		

the needs of all learners. Your use of course resources to inform the activity indicates thoughtful selection and connections to the selected standard. To further enhance this, consider adding methods for ongoing assessment during the lesson to track student progress and adjust instruction as needed.

The third example (Table 20) utilizes a restaurant menu format in which PSTs engage with short warm-up tasks (appetizers), a task that requires application of content and/or skills in a more substantive task (main dish), and additional smaller tasks that push PSTs to apply their skills and knowledge (side dishes). In the example below, the appetizers provide an opportunity for PSTs to critique specific elements (activities, standards and outcomes alignment, opportunities for differentiation) of a pre-created unit plan. The main dish options provide opportunities for PSTs to create an additional lesson plan for the unit that either scaffolds student background knowledge, implements cross-disciplinary learning, or further builds on a standard addressed within the unit. Finally, the side dishes give PSTs an opportunity to create a specific activity, assessment, or resource that could be added to the unit plan or to improve the clarity of a lesson within the unit plan through more explicit teacher directions, examples, or other resources. This menu project is aligned with InTASC Standards (CCSSO, 2011) and focuses on elements that fall within the "Essential Knowledge" category.

The rubric for this menu project is a weighted menu that utilizes proficiency language to assess PST tasks (Table 21). In utilizing this rubric, I provide PSTs with an opportunity to revise each assignment based on the feedback they receive on the first submission. For a submission of a cross-curricular lesson plan (main dish) that is assessed as "Approaching Target" in "Application of Instructional Strategy or Activity," feedback could state, "The strategy is relevant, but the explanation lacks some depth in terms of how it will support diverse learners. A more thorough integration of the instructional strategy with the pedagogical theory could enhance the clarity of its potential effectiveness. Expanding on how this strategy can foster engagement or scaffold learning would bring this closer to the target." For this same assignment that is assessed as "Approaching Target" in "Application to Practice," feedback might say,

While the connection to practice is present, it lacks sufficient real-world examples or detailed scenarios. Including specific examples of how students will interact with the content during the lesson and how assessments will be used to gauge learning would make the connection to practice clearer.

Table 20 Menu Example

Directions: Locate an existing unit plan consisting of at least four lessons for use with this activity. The unit plan can be for a grade level of your choice. Select one appetizer, one main dish, and two side dishes from this menu (one from each row) to complete utilizing the unit plan you selected. You may complete each activity in your choice of format or modality as long as the completed product meets the stated expectations.

Appetizers (choose one; 15% of assignment grade) InTASC Standard 1(d): The teacher understands how learning occurs—how learners construct knowledge, acquire skills, and develop disciplined thinking processes—and knows how to use instructional strategies that promote student learning.		
Assess the activities within the unit plan to determine if they are developmentally appropriate for the intended age/grade level of student. Support your assessment with appropriate sources.	Select one instructional strategy or activity within the unit plan and explain how this strategy may promote student learning within the lesson. Support your assessment with appropriate sources.	If the unit plan does not include specific strategies for differentiation, develop one potential differentiation strategy for students with varying learning needs, English language learners, or students with physical disabilities. Support your modification with appropriate sources.
Main Dish (choose one; 45% of assignment grade) InTASC Standard 7(k): The teacher knows a range of evidence-based instructional strategies, resources, and technological tools and how to use them effectively to plan instruction that meets diverse learning needs.		
Identify the knowledge students would need to have before engaging in the selected unit plan. Create a lesson that could be used to scaffold students' knowledge before engaging with the unit plan. This lesson plan should use the same format as the rest of the unit plan and include all the same sections.	Identify an opportunity for a cross-curricular lesson within this unit plan. Create a lesson plan that could be integrated with this unit plan but purposefully integrates a different content area. This lesson plan should use the same format as the rest of the unit plan and include all the same sections.	Select one of the standards and its corresponding student learning outcome. Create your own lesson plan to support students in meeting the stated learning outcome. This lesson plan should use the same format as the rest of the unit plan and include all the same sections.

Side Dish (choose one from each row; each is 20% of assignment grade)
Row 1—InTASC Standard 6(k): The teacher understands the range of types and multiple purposes of assessment and how to design, adapt, or select appropriate assessments to address specific learning goals and individual differences and minimize sources of bias.
Row 2—InTASC Standard 8(n): The teacher knows how to use a wide variety of resources, including human and technological, to engage students in learning.

Create a series of 10 open-ended questions that could be integrated into the lesson. Among the 10 questions, at least four levels of Bloom's taxonomy should be evident. Label each question according to the appropriate level(s) of Bloom's taxonomy.	Develop a project-based assessment that could be utilized as a summative assessment for this unit. Include the assessment's alignment with standards and student learning outcomes within the unit as well as grading criteria for the completed project.	Create a graphic organizer or other scaffolding tool that could be used by a student who needs additional support engaging with the information within the unit plan. Include both a blank version of the graphic organizer with instructions for use and a completed sample graphic organizer.
Locate an additional informational resource that could be integrated into the unit plan (text, video, website, primary resource). Explain how this additional resource could be utilized to support students' learning within the unit, the resource's alignment with stated student learning outcomes, and one activity that could be utilized to engage the students with the resource.	Create a cooperative activity to engage students with the content of the unit plan. The activity should be clearly aligned with at least one of the standards and student learning outcomes for the unit and should include student-friendly directions, individual expectations for participation, and a clear product/outcome from the activity.	Expand at least one of the lessons within the unit plan to include more explicit details for the teacher. This should include at least three of the following: scripting potential language for instruction, additional examples and non-examples, a unit pre-assessment of student knowledge, a formative assessment specific to one section of the unit, or an extension activity for students who master the information quickly.

Table 21 Rubric for Menu Choice Board

Criteria	Weight	Above Target (4)	Meets Target (3)	Approaching Target (2)	Below Target (1)
Alignment to InTASC standard	25%	The task demonstrates a deep and nuanced understanding of the relevant InTASC standard, with a clear and sophisticated application of its core principles or concepts.	The task clearly demonstrates an understanding of the relevant InTASC standard, showing a solid connection to its core principles or concepts.	The task demonstrates a basic understanding of the relevant InTASC standard, but the connection to the core principles or concepts is weak or unclear.	The task does not reflect an understanding of the relevant InTASC standard; there is little or no connection to the core principles or concepts from the standard.
Application of instructional strategy or activity	30%	Innovative or evidence-based strategy or activity is highly relevant, with a deep, well-justified connection to pedagogy and student learning.	Strategy or activity is relevant, well explained, and integrated with pedagogy, demonstrating its efficacy.	Strategy or activity is somewhat relevant but needs more explanation or integration with pedagogy.	Strategy or activity is irrelevant or misaligned or lacks justification.

Depth of content and pedagogical knowledge	30%	Comprehensive understanding of content and pedagogy with detailed examples that demonstrate mastery and advanced pedagogical insights.	Solid understanding of content and pedagogy with relevant examples, demonstrating an effective use of pedagogy.	Adequate understanding of content and pedagogy with basic examples but lacking in depth or detail.	Limited understanding of content and pedagogy; lacks supporting examples.
Application to practice	15%	Strong, detailed connection between theory and practice with multiple real-world examples, demonstrating expert application.	Clear connection between theory and practice with detailed examples from real classroom settings.	Some connection between theory and practice but lacks clarity or depth.	No clear connection between theory and practice; unclear explanation of how strategy works.

Additionally, explaining how you would adapt the lesson based on students' responses or engagement could strengthen the practical application.

The rubrics for choice boards (and many other tasks in my courses) also serve as a tool for the PSTs to self-evaluate their work and reflect on its effectiveness as a demonstration of how they have met proficiency of the stated objectives. I often ask PSTs to submit a completed rubric with their first task from any menu project to encourage this reflection while also providing me with an opportunity to see if there are parts of the rubric that are unclear and provide clarity.

The choice boards used in my courses are truly dynamic documents; tasks are added, refined, or removed across semesters based on feedback and ideas from PSTs. PSTs in my courses are actively invited to bring their ideas for tasks to me, where we will discuss their idea, negotiate guidelines, and write up the results of our discussion to make sure both I and the PST are clear on expectations for any newly created tasks. I also ask permission to use and adapt their task idea for future course sections. This has led to PSTs taking advantage of the opportunity to create and negotiate tasks with me, taking more ownership of their learning while also providing me with opportunities to learn from and with my PSTs through tasks that are specific to their context, such as their practicum placements. For example, one PST's practicum placement was in a school that had just adopted a new reading curriculum. As part of this adoption, teachers were engaging in weekly professional learning community meetings to prepare for upcoming lessons in the new curriculum. The PST wanted to engage in these meetings and use the experience to apply what she was learning in K–8 language arts methods. We discussed the possible tasks and formats that could be utilized and agreed to a series of reflective journal entries (one per week across eight weeks) and identified what should be included within these to meet the target learning objectives.

Reflection and Discussion Questions

"As a Teacher Educator" reflection questions are for the course instructor to reflect on their utilization of differentiated instruction. "As a Learner" and "As an Educator" questions are for PSTs to reflect on their experience with differentiation as a learner and how they can apply that experience to their future classrooms. The two sets of questions consider the dual roles of PSTs in the teacher educator program. It is recommended that PSTs have an opportunity to reflect on these questions individually before sharing and discussing them with peers.

As a Teacher Educator:

1. How can/do you ensure that the differentiated product options you assign are aligned with the standards and outcomes for your course?
2. Based on your PSTs' feedback regarding your use of product differentiation, did you effectively balance the cognitive, time, and resource demands of the various task choices you made available?
3. How do you communicate the objectives of each task clearly to PSTs to ensure that they understand the expectations and relevance to their learning and/or future practice?
4. What criteria did you use to help you design tasks across modalities while remaining focused on PSTs' ability to demonstrate growth or proficiency in the selected standard/objective?
5. In what ways do you gather and incorporate PST voice when designing differentiated task options?
6. How did your rubric design (e.g., single point vs. analytic) influence the level and type of feedback you provided? How did this, in turn, impact PST learning?
7. How do you encourage PSTs to reflect on their learning process and outcomes after completing their chosen tasks?
8. How do you evaluate whether a specific use of product differentiation in your class is effectively supporting student knowledge and growth?
9. What factors lead you to revise or refine differentiated task options for use in future classes?

As a Learner:

1. How did the opportunity to select which task(s) you completed to show your knowledge impact your motivation or engagement with the task itself?
2. What factor(s) influenced your choice of tasks to complete?
3. Do you feel the task(s) you chose to complete allowed you to communicate your knowledge and learning effectively? Explain.
4. What did you notice about the engagement of your peers in the choice task?

5   Did the various tasks available feel balanced? (Did it feel like they all require the same amount of time and effort?)
6   How did feedback on your work influence your learning? What type of feedback was most helpful?
7   How did your instructor's organization, scaffolding, and feedback support your learning during this assignment? What specific practices stood out as effective?
8   What did you learn about yourself as a learner through this differentiated assignment?
9   Reflecting on the diversity of your peers' needs and choices, how did this assignment foster an inclusive learning environment?

As an Educator:

1   How did experiencing product differentiation as a learner shape your understanding of its potential benefits and challenges in the classroom?
2   What considerations will you prioritize when designing differentiated products for your future students? How will you ensure that choices are equitable and aligned with learning objectives?
3   How will you incorporate scaffolding into product differentiation to meet the needs of all learners, including those who may struggle or excel?
4   How will you address the potential challenges of ensuring equity when designing differentiated assignments for students with varying needs, abilities, and resources?
5   What assessment tools (e.g., rubrics, formative feedback) do you see as most effective for evaluating differentiated products, and why?
6   How will you gather and use student feedback to refine your differentiated assignments in future teaching?
7   How does product differentiation connect to broader instructional strategies, such as Universal Design for Learning or culturally responsive teaching?
8   How might the diversity of your peers' experiences with product differentiation influence your approach to creating similar opportunities in your future classroom?
9   What strategies will you use to evaluate whether your future students feel that product differentiation is meaningful, equitable, and supportive of their learning goals?

7 Differentiated Instruction Across the Teacher Education Program: Building Faculty Capacity

In order for preservice teachers (PSTs) to get a full and rich understanding of differentiation through multiple models and opportunities for reflection, it is important that differentiated instruction (DI) is woven throughout the teacher education program (TEP) and not siloed within a single course (Shareefa, 2023). Integration of DI throughout the TEP provides PSTs with opportunities to see strategies modeled across content areas and by multiple instructors who may use different tools and strategies to support the needs of the diverse PSTs in their courses or who may explain these tools in different ways. In addition, the inclusion of DI throughout the TEP avoids reinforcing perceptions of DI as an "add-on" and instead shows how it is purposefully woven into one's teaching practice in various content areas and grade levels. Below are some strategies for supporting purposeful integration of DI throughout the TEP. These begin with a focus on faculty and program development and then branch out into opportunities for engagement with school partners who host PSTs in clinical placements.

Faculty Development

In order for TEP faculty to successfully implement DI into their coursework, they must have a solid knowledge foundation. As is the case with in-service teachers, there may be faculty within the program who do not feel confident or comfortable enacting DI within their teaching practice due to a lack of knowledge or resources (Preston et al., 2025). Thus, building faculty capacity is a vital first step for successful program-wide implementation of DI.

Program-Level Professional Learning Communities

Engaging faculty in professional learning communities (PLCs) is one approach to ongoing professional development that can be utilized to support both professional learning and interdisciplinary collaboration. PLCs are defined as organized small groups of educators with common interests or goals who work together to increase their knowledge and improve their teaching and are supported by a facilitator in this endeavor (Kosanovich & Foorman, 2016). This sort of ongoing professional development is effective for supporting faculty collaboration (Lay, 2024; Whinnery et al., 2020) and reducing feelings of isolation (Lay, 2024) in addition to providing opportunities for improving teaching (Kasanovich & Foorman, 2016) and program curriculum (Whinnery et al., 2020). TEP faculty note that PLCs and similar professional development structures require administrative support and opportunities for innovation to be effective (Lay, 2024).

Tap into Faculty Expertise

Another approach that acknowledges the expertise among faculty within the program is to invite faculty who are effectively implementing aspects of DI within their courses to present their strategies to colleagues. I have found that this is even more powerful if one or two PSTs from the course take part in the presentation to share their insights on how the DI strategies support their learning and will impact their own instruction. Depending on faculty schedules and comfort level, inviting faculty to observe a colleague who is implementing DI and following up with a debrief meeting in which faculty discuss what they observed and the enacting faculty member shares their planning and implementation process is another approach that leverages the good work already being done by faculty within the program.

This approach can be expanded by inviting faculty who are effectively implementing DI strategies in their courses to serve in coach or mentor roles for faculty who desire to build their skills and knowledge in this area. These mentor–mentee relationships can be structured through formalized peer coaching programs where faculty members engage in regular observation, co-planning, and reflective discussions on DI implementation. Peer teaching reviews can also push TEP faculty to engage in deeper reflection inspired by their observations of and discussion with peers (Preston et al., 2025). Organizing other structures, such as instructional rounds in which faculty get to observe a variety of colleagues' courses (Millington, 2025), can also be utilized to build faculty knowledge and provide opportunities for collaboration. Providing dedicated time and institutional support for these faculty partnerships, such as stipends or professional development credit, can further enhance faculty engagement and investment in the process.

Additionally, this model can create opportunities for cross-course and interdisciplinary collaboration, allowing faculty to explore how DI strategies function across different content areas and teaching contexts. By engaging as mentors or coaches, experienced faculty not only strengthen their own pedagogical expertise through reflective practice but also contribute to a culture of shared curricular leadership and innovation within the program. This structure helps to decentralize expertise, positioning DI not as an isolated initiative but as an integrated and evolving part of the program's instructional framework.

To further support the effectiveness of this approach, TEPs can provide structured mentorship training focused on coaching strategies, constructive feedback, and adult learning principles. Establishing clear goals and accountability measures—such as progress reflections, teaching portfolios, or group debrief sessions—can ensure that both mentors and mentees gain meaningful professional growth from the experience. Over time, this model can contribute to the development of a sustainable, faculty-led PLC that continually enhances the quality of instruction and student learning outcomes.

Engage Guest Experts

Invite guest speakers or DI experts to share best practices and innovative approaches. While there may be faculty within the program who have expertise and ideas to share with their colleagues, it can also be valuable to invite guest speakers to support faculty in implementation of DI. This can include whole-group training, interactive workshops, panel discussions, and small-group or individual consultations that allow faculty to identify specific

DI strategies appropriate for their courses and context. I have engaged in similar opportunities for professional development that provided me the opportunity to bring documents like my syllabus and a couple of major assignments to a one-on-one meeting with a guest expert and use that information to identify specific strategies and materials that could enhance student learning and engagement while also supporting course learning outcomes. These personalized consultations allowed me to receive tailored feedback and practical recommendations that directly applied to my course materials. Additionally, guest speakers often bring fresh perspectives, research-based strategies, and real-world examples that can help faculty refine their approach to DI. These guest speakers can include teachers from partner schools and districts, and program alumni. See below for more ideas for engaging the expertise of school partners in faculty professional development.

Furthermore, bringing in experts can help bridge the gap between theory and practice by demonstrating how DI techniques can be effectively implemented in various disciplines and class formats, including in-person, hybrid, and online learning environments. Faculty members can also gain insights into new assessment strategies, ways to scaffold instruction for diverse learners, and methods to leverage technology for differentiation.

By learning from and with external experts, faculty not only expand their professional networks but also cultivate a culture of continuous improvement and pedagogical innovation. This ongoing engagement can lead to long-term enhancements in teaching effectiveness and student success, reinforcing the importance of DI as a dynamic and responsive approach to education.

Provide Resources

Another way to support faculty development in implementation of DI is to provide resources such as research articles, case studies, lesson plans, or video examples showcasing DI in action. If faculty schedules or other constraints make it difficult to observe DI in action in the classrooms of colleagues and pre-K–12 partners, analysis and discussion of other resources can provide opportunities for faculty to gain a greater understanding of how to plan for and implement DI within the classroom. See below for more suggestions on building a collection of resources for this purpose.

Program Design

Explicit inclusion of DI within the TEP is another important step for effective implementation program-wide. To adapt the old adage, if it isn't in writing, it will not happen. Purposeful inclusion of DI into program documents, such as program learning outcomes and common language in course syllabi, as well as integration of DI into assessments of PST learning and proficiency, is one way to ensure that all program stakeholders see DI as an integral part of the TEP. Many national organizations' teaching preparation standards include explicit mention of differentiating instruction to meet the needs of diverse learners, including InTASC (performance standards 6(g) and 7(b) and essential knowledge standard 8(l); CCSSO, 2011), the Association for Advancing Quality in Educator Preparation (standard 1a; AAQEP, 2025), and the Council for Accreditation of Educator Preparation (standards 3.d and 4.f; CAEP, 2018), as do content-specific organizations, such as the International Literacy Association (standards 2.4 and 5.2; ILA, 2017) and the National Science Teaching Association (standard 2b; NSTA, 2020). Thus, programs seeking accreditation through these or other national organizations will need to provide evidence that their completers are knowledgeable about strategies for DI and the application of these strategies in the classroom. State educator preparation standards also often include specific mention of candidates' ability to utilize strategies for DI, as is the case in Montana, where I currently work to support PSTs.

Infuse DI into Programmatic Course Mapping

Including DI-related competencies and practices in course mapping within the TEP provides opportunities to create a cohesive and scaffolded learning experience for PSTs, ensuring that they engage with DI in meaningful and developmentally appropriate ways throughout their program. By systematically embedding DI across coursework, PSTs can progressively build their understanding, from foundational theories to advanced application, while receiving targeted support and feedback throughout their program.

This approach requires faculty collaboration to determine where DI is best introduced, reinforced, and mastered within the program. Faculty can work together to align course objectives, assignments, and assessments with DI principles, ensuring that PSTs revisit and deepen their knowledge over time.

Additionally, integrating DI into course mapping allows for cross-course connections, enabling faculty to plan for the integration of DI and helping PSTs see how differentiation applies across content areas, student needs, and instructional settings.

Integrate DI into Program Assignments and Assessments

Design shared assignments or projects (e.g., lesson planning with DI) that are implemented and assessed across multiple courses. This can include major assignments that are utilized in multiple courses to provide opportunities for PSTs to engage in DI practices, receive feedback on their implementation (or planning for such), and reflect on these experiences. These assignments can be scaffolded across semesters and courses to provide chances for PSTs to show their growth in planning and implementing DI as well. For example, in one program I have worked in, PSTs create a draft thematic lesson sequence early in their program. This unit plan is revised throughout their coursework and becomes their capstone project. Although the first draft includes information on differentiation strategies in the lessons, PSTs are expected to actively reflect on and revise the strategies included as they engage in additional coursework. This project was developed by the instructors in the program collaboratively, with some areas of the unit plan being refined in specific courses (such as pedagogical methods being refined in the appropriate methods course), while others (such as differentiation and student engagement) are woven throughout the program in multiple courses.

Integrate DI into Clinical Placements

Include DI as a core component of clinical placement evaluations (both practicum and student teaching) and feedback. This will require the TEP to ensure that mentor teachers and/or university field supervisors are trained to observe and assess PSTs' implementation of DI and to provide targeted feedback to support PSTs' professional development in this area. This can be facilitated through purposeful inclusion of differentiation within observation rubrics that explicitly address PSTs' ability to plan and implement DI within their clinical placement classrooms. Such rubrics should be aligned with both program learning outcomes and relevant accreditation or other standards to ensure that DI remains an area in which PSTs receive growth-focused feedback throughout their clinical experiences.

In addition, TEPs can provide structured opportunities for reflection on the implementation of DI within clinical placements. This can include tailored journal prompts, reflective analysis in which PSTs view videos of their lessons and reflect on their use of DI, and small-group debriefs in which PSTs discuss the successes and the challenges they have experienced as they implemented DI within their clinical placements. TEPs can also encourage PSTs to collect and analyze student work samples to help them consider how DI implementation may impact the learners in their classrooms. This type of analysis can be further supported through scaffolded action research within the program.

Interdisciplinary Collaboration

As mentioned previously, engaging in interdisciplinary opportunities for engaging in differentiation within the TEP program will provide PSTs with an increased understanding of how DI can be applied across content areas. This can include collaboration with instructors from other departments that PSTs engage with for content area and elective courses. If your college or university has a center or office that supports faculty professional development, leveraging this resource to engage faculty across campus in learning about and enacting DI could be a valuable approach to further demonstrating application of DI for PSTs (and other students in higher education).

Creating opportunities for faculty from different disciplines to co-teach or plan integrated units that incorporate DI enhances PSTs' ability to see differentiation as a flexible and adaptive practice, relevant across all subject areas. Such collaborations may take a variety of forms, including guest teaching, semester-long co-teaching, and interdisciplinary PLCs. Faculty can also work together to design cross-disciplinary assignments that require PSTs to apply DI strategies in multiple content areas. For example, a science methods instructor and a special education faculty member might collaborate on an assignment where PSTs develop a differentiated lab activity that considers students' varying readiness levels, learning needs, and interests. Similarly, an English professor and an education faculty member could codesign a unit where PSTs analyze diverse texts through the lens of differentiation, examining how literature selections and instructional approaches can be adapted to support all learners.

Additionally, hosting campus-wide workshops, faculty panels, or DI-focused discussion groups can create further opportunities for interdisciplinary collaboration. These initiatives not only strengthen faculty's ability to integrate DI into their own instruction but also reinforce for PSTs that differentiation is a widely applicable practice, essential for meeting the diverse needs of learners in any subject area. By embedding interdisciplinary DI experiences throughout the program, TEPs can help PSTs build a strong foundation in responsive teaching that will carry over into their future classrooms.

Modeling and Practice

It is important to provide opportunities for PSTs to see DI explicitly modeled. The same is true in supporting TEP faculty as they expand their own knowledge and implementation of DI in their courses. This can include explicit modeling of DI strategies in faculty professional development activities as well as observations of colleagues who are effectively utilizing DI strategies. Structured peer observations, followed by guided discussions or collaborative reflections, can help faculty identify effective differentiation techniques and consider how to apply them in their own teaching.

Another way to support faculty in developing their knowledge and implementation of DI is through opportunities for microteaching or simulations where program faculty practice DI with peers or in virtual environments. Faculty can engage in lesson studies, where they design a lesson incorporating DI, teach it in a low-stakes setting, and receive feedback from colleagues on the effectiveness of their strategies. Virtual teaching simulations, where faculty interact with AI-driven student avatars that respond in real time, can also provide an opportunity to test differentiation strategies and refine instructional approaches before applying them in their courses. Such simulations can be particularly beneficial in helping faculty anticipate and respond to diverse learning needs, experiment with various scaffolding techniques, and practice making real-time adjustments to instruction based on student responses. Additionally, incorporating video analysis into microteaching sessions (where faculty record, review, and reflect on their own DI) can further enhance self-awareness and professional growth.

Provide Resources

Among the obstacles to effective implementation of DI is a lack of knowledge and resources (Altun & Nayman, 2022). Even with increased faculty knowledge, there will still be a need for access to resources that provide examples and ideas for implementing DI across content areas. These resources can be sourced from a variety of sources, including research from scholarly journals, professional resource books, publications (both digital and hard copy) from professional organizations, and materials created by both faculty and PSTs in the program. These materials can include templates, lesson plans, and digital tools. Consider working with your institution's library to make resources created within the program accessible digitally to faculty, PSTs, and even teachers in partner schools. These shared resources can serve as a growing repository of practical strategies, fostering a culture of continuous learning and adaptation. Additionally, faculty can encourage PSTs to contribute case studies and sample differentiated activities to this collection, further enriching its relevance and usefulness. Establishing a system for regularly updating and curating these resources ensures that they remain aligned with evolving research and best practices. Partnering with local schools and educators to gather feedback on the usability and effectiveness of these materials can also enhance their impact, creating a dynamic exchange between theory and practice.

Many programs have regular communications with faculty and staff, such as newsletters or e-mail updates. These communications are another opportunity to share research and evidence-based practices for DI and to provide a space for faculty to share their ideas for DI implementation. This could be through a short column written by a faculty member to share a strategy they have implemented successfully, a spotlight feature highlighting innovative DI practices within the program, or a suggested resource for faculty to explore. Newsletters might also include a Q&A section where faculty can submit questions about DI and receive expert insights or peer responses. This interactive element allows for direct engagement and helps address real-time concerns or barriers to implementation. Incorporating multimedia elements, such as short video clips or recorded mini-workshops, can provide faculty with engaging and accessible professional development opportunities. Additionally, these newsletters or e-mail updates can include testimonials from or interviews with faculty members who have experimented with DI approaches, sharing their successes, challenges, and lessons learned. This peer-driven content fosters a sense of community and encourages open dialogue about best practices, making DI a more integral part of the teaching culture. Regularly including DI content in these communications ensures that faculty stay engaged with ongoing professional development and have a steady stream of new strategies and resources.

Partnerships and Clinical Placements

One of the greatest assets for any TEP can be the pre-K–12 schools with which they partner for PSTs' clinical placements, research opportunities, and other collaboration with the expert teachers within them. These partnerships provide valuable, real-world contexts for PSTs and teacher educators to observe and engage with DI in action. School administrators and teachers are often able to identify colleagues or teacher teams who are effectively implementing elements of DI within their own classrooms. Depending on the teachers' level of comfort, space constraints, and the relationship between the TEP and school, there may be multiple opportunities for PSTs to engage with DI in authentic settings. This could include placements in the classrooms of expert teachers, scheduled class visits for PSTs to observe DI in action, or even guest lectures by in-service teachers who can share their experiences with differentiation and offer practical insights into their instructional decision-making.

To extend the learning from these opportunities to engage with in-service teachers around strategies for differentiation, it is also important to provide structured reflection opportunities for faculty. Facilitating reflective discussions, guided debriefs, or structured journaling activities allows TEP faculty to process what they observed and connect it to the courses they teach. Engaging in collaborative reflections in which multiple faculty members share their observations and insights encourages critical thinking and a deeper analysis of DI strategies. This process can also help challenge preconceived notions or biases about differentiation by exposing faculty to diverse perspectives and interpretations.

Reflection and Discussion Questions

"As a Teacher Educator" reflection questions in this chapter are for the course instructor to reflect on their utilization of DI, how their program supports them in building their knowledge of DI, and how DI is implemented across their TEP. "As a Learner" and "As an Educator" questions are for PSTs to reflect on their experience with differentiation across the TEP and how they can apply that experience to their future classrooms. The two sets of questions consider the dual roles of PSTs in the TEP. It is recommended that PSTs have an opportunity to reflect on these questions individually before sharing and discussing them with peers.

As a Teacher Educator:

1. How do we define differentiation within our TEP?
2. What assumptions do instructors in our TEP hold about the challenges and benefits of DI for PSTs?
3. How is DI being introduced and reinforced across our TEP?
4. How do we scaffold PSTs' understanding and implementation of DI over the course of their program?
5. How is DI currently represented within your program's learning outcomes, syllabi, and assessments? What changes could be made to ensure that DI is explicitly woven throughout the program?
6. How do instructors in our TEP work together to integrate DI throughout the program?
7. What interdisciplinary collaboration opportunities exist within your institution to model DI across content areas? How could these collaborations benefit both faculty and PSTs?
8. How can we ensure consistency in DI language, strategies, and expectations across courses and faculty?
9. How do we address varied levels of faculty comfort and expertise with DI?
10. How do we assess PSTs' ability to design and implement DI strategies in their fieldwork and student teaching?
11. What feedback do we receive from mentor teachers or partner schools about our candidates' preparedness to differentiate instruction?
12. What data do we need to gather to evaluate the effectiveness of our DI integration efforts?
13. How does our TEP's implementation of DI align with our goals for equity and inclusion in the program?

14 How confident do you feel in your own knowledge and implementation of DI in your courses? What areas do you feel you need additional support or resources in?

15 In what ways have you observed or experienced DI being implemented effectively in higher-education settings? How might those strategies be adapted for your own teaching?

16 What professional learning opportunities, such as PLCs or faculty mentorship, would be most beneficial for enhancing your ability to integrate DI into your courses?

17 How can you contribute to a faculty learning community focused on DI? What expertise or experiences could you share with your colleagues?

As a Learner:

1 What types of differentiation (content, process, product, learning environment) have I observed across courses in my TEP? How have these strategies impacted my engagement and understanding?

2 Have I noticed differences in how my instructors model DI? What approaches seem most effective, and why?

3 How has my understanding of DI evolved throughout my coursework?

4 How have my TEP courses helped me develop the skills and confidence to differentiate instruction in my future classroom?

5 What connections can I make between DI and other instructional approaches I have studied (e.g., culturally responsive teaching, Universal Design for Learning, inquiry-based learning)?

6 What feedback have I received on my lesson plans and teaching demonstrations regarding differentiation? How have I adjusted my approach based on this feedback?

7 What role has reflection played in shaping my understanding of DI? How do I plan to continue this reflective practice as an educator?

8 Have I been given opportunities to design and revise lessons that incorporate DI? What have I learned from this process?

9 How have assignments in different courses allowed me to practice planning for and implementing DI? Where do I feel most prepared, and where do I need more growth?

10 How have my experiences in interdisciplinary coursework or co-teaching opportunities influenced my understanding of differentiation across content areas?

11 If I were designing my TEP experience, what additional experiences, resources, or coursework would I include to strengthen my ability to differentiate instruction?

As an Educator:

1 Which of the strategies I have experienced in my TEP do I want to incorporate into my own teaching practice?

2 Have I had the opportunity to plan or implement a lesson with differentiation? If so, what went well, and what would I do differently next time?

3 How can collaboration with my mentor teacher, university supervisor, or fellow PSTs help me develop my DI skills?

4 What resources or professional development opportunities might help me strengthen my ability to differentiate instruction?

Appendix A: Graphic Organizer for Utilization of the Dual Role Reflection Model

Directions: The purpose of this graphic organizer is to support you in deeply exploring a single reflection prompt or classroom experience from multiple perspectives. Follow the steps below to guide your thinking and analysis.

1. Select one of the reflection prompts from those provided or consider a recent classroom experience and briefly summarize it.

2. Reflect on the question as a learner and as an educator. "As a Learner" prompts provide you with an opportunity to consider the prompt or experience as someone receiving instruction in the classroom, while "As an Educator" prompts provide you with an opportunity to reflect on the prompt or experience as someone who is or will be delivering instruction.

3. Use the prompts in the first column to help you consider the question from multiple perspectives. These include the following:

    a. In My Experience: Pull from your own personal experiences in your coursework and clinical placements as well as your experiences as a student in other settings, such as K–12 school.

    b. In the Desks: Consider the perspectives of other students in the classroom, including those of your peers in the classroom.

    c. In the Profession: Reflect on the prompt or experience as it applies to the teaching profession.

4. After completing the organizer, review your reflections to identify patterns or themes. How does your thinking as a learner shape your approach as an educator? How might your reflections in both roles influence your decisions as a teacher?

5. Be ready to share key takeaways in discussion with peers and complete the synthesis question below this organizer.

Reflection Prompt

Perspective	As a Learner		As an Educator	
In My Experience	Considering my own learning, engagement, needs, goals, self-efficacy		Considering my application and adaptation of content and its relevance	
In the Desks	Considering my peers' learning, engagement, needs, goals, self-efficacy		Considering my students' learning, engagement, needs, goals, self-efficacy	
In the Profession	Considering my teacher's knowledge, strategies, instructional choices		Considering my pedagogical knowledge, strategies, instructional choices	

Final synthesis question: How do your experiences as a learner influence your approach as an educator, and how might my understanding as an educator reshape the way you engage with learning in the future? What insights from both roles can you apply to better support diverse learners in my classroom?

Appendix B: Synthesis Reflection Questions for Instructors and Preservice Teachers

Reflection and Discussion Questions

"As a Teacher Educator" reflection questions are for the course instructor to reflect on their utilization of differentiated instruction (DI) across the semester. "As a Learner" and "As an Educator" questions are for preservice teachers (PSTs) to reflect on their experience with differentiation as a learner and how they can apply that experience to their future classrooms. The two sets of questions consider the dual roles of PSTs in the teacher educator program. It is recommended that PSTs have an opportunity to reflect on these questions individually before sharing and discussing them with peers. PST reflection questions in this appendix will focus on their experiences across the semester and throughout their TEP and will push them to consider their future application of DI holistically.

As a Teacher Educator:

1. In what ways have I intentionally differentiated instruction to meet the diverse needs of PSTs in my courses this semester?
2. How have I modeled DI strategies in my teaching, ensuring that PSTs experience differentiation as learners?
3. What evidence do I have that the strategies I utilized for differentiation were effective in meeting PSTs' varying needs, backgrounds, and experiences?
4. How have PSTs in my courses responded to my differentiation strategies? What feedback have they provided, either formally or informally?
5. What were the biggest challenges I faced when differentiating instruction? How did I address or attempt to address them?
6. Based on this semester, what adjustments will I make to improve my use of differentiation next term?

7 How can I better model differentiation as a practice that PSTs should carry into their own classrooms?

8 What steps can I take to ensure that differentiation is embedded throughout my course rather than as an occasional strategy?

9 If I were a PST in my course, how would I experience differentiation? Would I feel supported, challenged, and engaged?

As a Learner:

1 How do you think the instructor decided which differentiation strategies to use in this course? What evidence of intentional planning and alignment with learning goals can you see?

2 If you could suggest one improvement to the differentiation strategies used in this course, what would it be? How do you think this change could enhance learning for you and your peers?

3 How did the opportunities for choice in learning (e.g., format, content, tasks) reflect the instructor's approach to differentiation? How might you adapt these strategies in your own teaching?

4 What did you notice about how the instructor gathered and utilized information about the prior knowledge and skills of you and your peers to adjust instruction? How does this modeling influence your understanding of the role of pre-assessment in DI?

5 How did the instructor adjust instruction or materials as the course progressed? How might this flexibility serve as a model for your future teaching?

6 How do you think the instructor evaluated the effectiveness of their differentiation strategies? In what ways did the instructor communicate this information with PSTs in their course? How might you adopt similar reflective practices when differentiating instruction in your future classroom?

7 How did the instructor model equitable practices through differentiation? How might these practices shape your approach to creating an inclusive classroom environment?

8 What have you learned from your peers' reflections or observations about differentiation strategies? How has this influenced your perspective as a future teacher?

9 How is differentiation woven into coursework throughout your teacher education program?

As an Educator:

1 How will you gather feedback from students and reflect on your practice to continually improve your differentiation strategies?

2 Which differentiation strategies from this course are you most excited to implement in your future classroom? How will you adapt these strategies to your subject area or grade level?

3 What challenges do you anticipate when implementing differentiation in your classroom? How will you address these challenges to ensure success?

4 How might you involve families in supporting differentiated learning experiences for their children?

5 How will you build relationships with your students to better understand their needs, interests, and backgrounds, and how will this knowledge inform your differentiation practices?

Appendix C: Preservice Teacher Questions for Reflecting on Differentiated Instruction within Clinical Placements

Reflection and Discussion Questions

"As a Learner" and "As an Educator" questions are for preservice teachers (PSTs) to reflect on their experience with differentiation as a learner and how they can apply that experience to their future classrooms. The two sets of questions consider the dual roles of PSTs in the teacher educator program. It is recommended that PSTs have an opportunity to reflect on these questions individually before sharing and discussing them with peers. PST reflection questions in this appendix will focus on their experiences within their clinical placements and will push them to consider their future application of differentiated instruction (DI) holistically.

As a Learner

1. What differentiation strategies have I observed in my clinical placements? How have they influenced my understanding of DI?
2. What differences have I noticed in differentiation strategies used across grade levels and content areas in my clinical placements?
3. Have I encountered students in my placement who needed additional support or enrichment? How did my mentor teacher address these needs?
4. How has feedback from my mentor teacher or university supervisor helped me refine my approach to differentiation?
5. What role does differentiation play in my mentor teacher's approach to classroom culture and student relationships?
6. How have I seen differentiation implemented in classrooms with high student diversity, including English language learners and students with learning differences?

7 Have I had opportunities to engage in reflective discussions about DI with my mentor teachers? What insights have I gained from these conversations?

8 What assumptions did I have about differentiation before entering my clinical placement? How have they changed based on my experiences?

As an Educator:

1 How have mentor teachers modeled DI in their classrooms? What aspects of their approach would I like to incorporate into my own teaching?

2 What challenges have I faced in implementing DI strategies during my clinical placements? How have I addressed them, or how might I handle them differently in the future?

3 How comfortable do I feel making real-time instructional adjustments to meet students' diverse needs? How can I continue building this skill?

4 How have I adapted assessments to accommodate students with different learning needs? What have I learned from this process?

5 How have students responded to differentiation strategies I have used? Have I noticed differences in engagement, participation, or learning outcomes?

6 How have I used student data (e.g., formative assessments, observations, work samples) to inform my differentiation strategies?

7 How do I plan to continue developing my skills in differentiation as I transition from a PST to an in-service teacher?

References

Al-Shehri, M. S. (2020). Effect of differentiated instruction on the achievement and development of critical thinking skills among sixth-grade science students. *International Journal of Learning, Teaching, and Educational Research, 19*, 77–99. https://doi.org/10.26803/ijlter.19.10.5

Altun, S., & Nayman, H. (2022). Differentiated instruction: A study on teachers' experiences and opinions. *International Online Journal of Education Sciences, 14*, 374–386.

American Psychological Association. (2019, May 30). Belief in learning styles myth may be detrimental. Accessed December 15, 2025, from https://www.apa.org/news/press/releases/2019/05/learning-styles-myth

Anderson, L., & Krathwol, D. (Eds.). (2001). *A taxonomy for learning, teaching, and assessing: A revision of Bloom's taxonomy of education objectives.* Pearson.

Angelo, T. A., & Cross, P. K. (1993). *Classroom assessment techniques* (2nd ed.). Jossey-Bass.

Asafova, E., & Vashetina, O. (2022). Goal-setting as a condition for professional self-development of master's students in teacher training programme. ARPHA Proceedings (5, 97–107). https://doi.org/10.3897/ap.5.e0097

Association for Advancing Quality in Teacher Preparation (AAQEP). (2025). 2025 Expectations Framework. Fairfax Station, VA. Accessed January 17, 2025, from https://aaqep.org/files/2025%20AAQEP%20Expectations%20Framework.pdf

Atjonen, P., Pöntinen, S., Kontkanen, S., & Ruotsalainen, P. (2022). In enhancing preservice teachers' assessment literacy: Focus on knowledge base, conceptions of assessment, and teacher learning. *Frontiers in Education, 7.* doi:10.3389/feduc.2022.891391

Ball, D. L., & Cohen, D. K. (1999). Developing practice, developing practitioners: Toward a practice-based theory of professional education. In L. Darling-Hammond & G. Skyes (Eds.), *Teaching as a learning profession: Handbook of policy and practice*, 3–32. Jossey-Bass.

Beauchamp, C. (2014). Reflection in teacher education: Issues emerging from a review of current literature. *Reflective Practice, 16*, 123–141. http://dx.doi.org/10.1080/14623943.2014.982525

Becker, A. (2016). Student-generated scoring rubrics: Examining their formative value for improving ESL students' writing performance. *Assessing Writing, 29*, 1524. https://doi.org/10.1016/j.asw.2016.05.002

Beymer, P. N., & Thomson, M. M. (2015). The effects of choice in the classroom: Is there too little or too much choice? *Support for Learning, 30*, 105–120. https://doi.org/10.1111/1467-9604.12086

Bogen, E. C., Schlendorf, C. P., Nicolino, P. A., & Morote, E. (2019). Instructional strategies in differentiated instruction for systemic change. *Journal for Leadership and Instruction, 18*, 18–22.

Bondie, R. S., Dahnke, C., & Zusho, A. (2019). How does changing "one-size-fits-all" to differentiated instruction affect teaching? *Review of Research in Education, 43*, 336–362. https://doi.org/10.3102/0091732X18821130

Boyd, D. (2012, May 25). Did camel riding help lower FCAT Writing scores? *The Gainesville Sun.* https://www.gainesville.com/story/news/2012/05/25/dan-boyd-did-camel-riding-help-lower-fcat-writing-scores/31835886007

Brunker, N., Spandagou, I., & Grice, C. (2019). Assessment for learning while learning to assess: Assessment in initial teacher education through the eyes of pre-service teachers and teacher educators. *Australian Journal of Teacher Education, 44*, Article 6. https://ro.ecu.edu.au/ajte/vol44/iss9/6

Cañadas, L. (2023). Contribution of formative assessment for developing teacher competences in education. *European Journal of Teacher Education, 46*, 516–532. https://doi.org/10.1080/02619768.2021.1950684

Chamberlin M., & Powers R. (2010). The promise of differentiated instruction for enhancing the mathematical understandings of college students. *Teaching Mathematics and Its Applications: An International Journal of the IMA, 29*(3), 113–139.

Clark, C. M., & Rust, F. O. (2006). Learning-centered assessment in teacher education. *Studies in Educational Evaluation, 32*, 73–82.

Clark, S. K., & Byrnes, D. (2015). What millennial preservice teachers want to learn in their training. *Journal of Early Childhood Teacher Educator, 36*, 379–395. https://doi.org/10.1080/10901027.2015.1100148

Conway, P. F. (2001). Anticipatory reflection while learning to teach: From a temporally truncated to a temporally distributed model of reflection in teacher education. *Teaching and Teacher Education, 17*, 89–106.

Cornelius, K. E. (2013). Formative assessment made easy: Templates for collecting daily data in inclusive classrooms. *Teaching Exceptional Children, 45*(5), 14–21.

Council for the Accreditation of Educator Preparation (CAEP). (2018). K–6 elementary teacher preparation standards [Initial licensure programs]. CAEP. Accessed from https://caepnet.org/~/media/Files/caep/standards/2018-caep-k-6-elementary-teacher-prepara.pdf?la=en

Council of Chief State School Officers. (2011, April). Interstate Teacher Assessment and Support Consortium (InTASC) Model Core Teaching Standards: A Resource for State Dialogue. Author.

Cuevas, J. (2015). Is learning styles-based instruction effective? A comprehensive analysis of recent research on learning styles. *Theory and Research in Education, 13*, 308–333. doi:10.1177/1477878515606621

Dack, H. (2018). Structuring teacher candidate learning about differentiated instruction through coursework. *Teaching and Teacher Education, 69*, 62–74. https://doi.org/10.1016/j.tate.2017.09.017

Dack, H. (2019). The role of teacher preparation program coherence in supporting candidate appropriation of the pedagogical tools of differentiated instruction. *Teaching and Teacher Education, 78*, 125–140. doi:10.1016.j.tate.2018.11.011

Dack, H., & Triplett, N. (2020). Novice social studies teachers' implementation of differentiation: A longitudinal multicase study. *Theory and Research in Social Education, 48*, 32–73. https://doi.org/10.1080/00933104.2019.1640149

Dack, H., Chiles, E., Kathman, L., Poessnecker, A., & Strohl, E. (2022). The key to equitable differentiation. *Middle School Journal, 53*, 15–32. https://doi.org/10.1080/00940771.2022.2119756

Danley, A. (2019). Using "start, stop, and continue" to gather student feedback to improve instruction. In A. deNoyelles, A. Albrecht, S. Bauer, & S. Wyatt (Eds.), *Teaching online pedagogical repository*. University of Central Florida Center for Distributed Learning. https://topr.online.ucf.edu/using-start-stop-and-continue-to-gather-student-feedback-to-improve-instruction.

deBettencourt, L. U., & Nagro, S. E. (2018). Tracking special education teacher candidates' reflective practices over time. *Remedial & Special Education, 40*, 277–288. https://doi.org/10.1177/0741932518762

De Neve, D., & Devos, G. (2015). The role of environmental factors in beginning teachers' professional learning related to differentiated instruction. *School Effectiveness and School Improvement, 27*, 357–379. https://doi.org/10.1080/09243453.2015.1122637

Diasti, K. S., Murniati, C. T., & Hartono, H. (2023). The implementation of KWL strategy in EFL students' reading comprehension. *Journal of English Teaching, 9*, 176–185. https://doi.org/10.33541/jet.v9i2.4676

D'Intino, J. S., & Wang, L. (2021). Differentiated instruction: A review of teacher education practices for Canadian pre-service elementary school teachers. *Journal of Education for Teaching, 47*, 668–681. https://doi.org/10.1080/02607476.2021.1951603

Dixon, F. A., Yssel, N., McConnell, J. M., & Hardin, T. (2014). Differentiated instruction, professional development, and teacher efficacy. *Journal for the Education of the Gifted, 37*(2), 111–127. https://doi.org/10.1177/0162353214529042

Dixson, D. D., & Worrell, F. C. (2016). Formative and summative assessment in the classroom. *Theory into Practice, 55*, 153–159. https://doi.org/10.1080/00405841.2016.1148989

Dnyanesh, S., Pattanshetti, S. V., Bhimalli, S. M., Dixit, & D. (2022). Jigsaw technique: An innovative teaching strategy in anatomy. *Journal of the Scientific Society, 49*, 322–325.

Doran, G. T. (1981). There's a S.M.A.R.T. way to write management's goals and objectives. *Management Review, 70*, 35–36.

Erdemire, N., & Yeşilçınar, S. (2021). Reflective practices in micro teaching from the perspective of preservice teachers: Teacher feedback, peer feedback and self-reflection. *Reflective Practice, 22*, 766–781. https://doi.org/10.1080/14623943.2021.1968818

Fluckiger, J. (2010). Single point rubric: A tool for responsible self-assessment. *Teacher Education Faculty Publications*, 5. https://digitalcommons.unomaha.edu/tedfacpub/5

Fraile, J., Panadero, E., & Pardo, R. (2017). Co-creating rubrics: The effects on self-regulated learning, self-efficacy and performance of establishing assessment criteria with students. *Studies in Educational Evaluation, 53*, 69–76. https://doi.org/10.1016/j.stueduc.2017.03.003

Gaitas, S., & Martins, M. A. (2017). Teacher perceived difficulty in implementing differentiated instructional strategies in primary school. *International Journal of Inclusive Education, 21*, 554–556. https://doi.org/10.1080/13603116.2016.1223180

Gao, S., Liu, K., & McKinney, M. (2019). Learning formative assessment in the field: Analysis of reflective conversations between preservice teachers and their classroom mentors. *International Journal of Mentoring and Coaching in Education, 8*, 197–216. https://doi.org/10.1108/IJMCE-10-2018-0056

Geisinger, K. F. (2016). 21st century skills: What are they and how do we assess them? *Applied Measurement in Education, 29*, 245–249. https://doi.org/10.1080/08957347.2016.1209207

Gheyssens, E., Griful-Freixenet, J., & Stuyven, K. (2020). Differentiated instruction as a student-centered teaching approach in higher education. In S. Hoidn & M. Klemeni (Eds.), *The Routledge international handbook of student-centered learning and teaching in higher education*, 254–268. Taylor & Francis. https://doi.org/10.1007/978-3-031-31678-4_30

Gibbs, G. (1988). *Learning by doing: A guide to teaching and learning methods*. Further Education Unit. Oxford Polytechnic.

Gibbs, K., & Beamish, W. (2021). Conversations with Australian teachers and school leaders about using differentiated instruction in a mainstream secondary school. *Australian Journal of Teacher Education, 46*, Article 6. http://dx.doi.org/10.14221/ajte.2021v46n7.6

Goddard, Y. L., Goddard, R. D., Bailes, L. P., & Nichols, R. (2019). From school leadership to differentiated instruction: A pathway to student learning. *The Elementary School Journal, 120*, 197–219.

Graham, L. J., de Bruin, K., Lassig, C., & Spandagou, I. (2021). A cropping review of 20 years of research on differentiation: Investigating conceptualization, characteristics, and methods used. *Review of Education, 9*, 161–198. https://doi.org/10.1002/rev3.3238

Hamodi, C., López-Pastor, V. M., & López-Pastor, A. T. (2017). If I experience formative assessment whilst studying at university, will I put it into practice later as a teacher? Formative and shared assessment in Initial Teacher Education (ITE). *European Journal of Teacher Education, 40*, 171–190. http://dx.doi.org/10.1080/02619768.2017.1281909

Hattie, J. (2024, November). *Concept mapping*. Corwin Visible Learning plus. https://www.visiblelearningmetax.com/influences/view/concept_mapping

Hatton, N., & Smith, D. (1995). Reflection in teacher education: Toward definition and implementation. *Teaching & Teacher Education, 11*, 33–49.

Hogg, L. (2016). Applying funds of knowledge theory in a New Zealand high school: New directions for pedagogical practice. *Teachers and Curriculum, 16*, 49–55.

Hong, H., Knollman, G., & Doran, P. R. (2022). Exploring alternative perspectives on millennial teachers' beliefs of and engagement with cultural and linguistic diversity: The use of reflective practice. *Reflective Practice, 23*, 409–421. https://doi.org/10.1080/14623943.2022.2040011

International Literacy Association (ILA). (2017). *Standards for the preparation of literacy professionals*. International Literacy Association.

Jager, L., Denessen, E., Cillessen, A., & Meijer, P. C. (2022). Capturing instructional differentiation in educational research: Investigating opportunities and challenges. *Educational Research, 64*, 224–241. https://doi.org/10.1080/00131881.2022.2063751

Johnson, C. C., Sondergeld, T. A., & Walton, J. B. (2019). A study of the implementation of formative assessment in three large urban districts. *American Educational Research Journal, 56*, 2408–2438. https://doi.org/10.3102/0002831219842347

Jones, M., & Ryan, J. (2014). Learning in the practicum: Engaging pre-service teachers in reflective practice in the online space. *Asia-Pacific Journal of Teacher Education, 42*, 132–146. https://doi.org/10.1080/1359866X.2014.892058

Jørgensen, M. T., & Brogaard, L. (2021). Using differentiated teaching to address academic diversity in higher education: Empirical evidence from two cases. *Learning and Teaching: The International Journal of Higher Education in the Social Sciences, 14*(2), 87–110. https://doi.org/10.3167/latiss.2021.140206

Joseph, S., Thomas, M., Simonette, G., & Ramsook, L. (2013). The impact of differentiated instruction in a teacher education setting: Successes and challenges. *International Journal of Higher Education, 2*, 28–40. http://dx.doi.org/10.5430/ijhe.v2n3p28

Kettler, T., & Taliaferro, C. (2022). *Personalizing learning in gifted education*. Prufrock Press.

Kieran, L., & Anderson, C. (2019). Connecting universal design for learning with culturally responsive teaching. *Education and Urban Society, 51*, 1202–1216. https://doi.org/10.1177/0013124518785012

Kim, S., Hur, Y., & Park, J. (2014). The correlation between achievement goals, learning strategies, and motivation in medical students. *Korean Journal of Medical Education, 26*(1), 19–24. https://doi.org/10.3946/kjme.2014.26.1.19

Kimpo, R., & Puder, B. (2023). A neuroanatomy lab practical exam format in alignment with the universal design for learning framework. *Anatomical Sciences Education, 16*(6), 1046–1057. https://doi.org/10.1002/ase.2316

Kings College. (2023). How is college different from high school? https://www.kings.edu/admissions/high_school_vs_college#:~:text=HIGH%20SCHOOL%3A%20You%20spend%20on,usually%20with%20breaks%20in%20between

Kofler, M. J., Singh, L. J., Soto, E. F., Chan, E. S. M., Miller, C. E., Harmon, S. L., & Spiegel, J. A. (2020). Working memory and short-term memory deficits in ADHD: A bifactor modeling approach. *Neuropsychology, 34*, 686–698. https://doi.org/10.1037/neu0000641

Kolb, D. A. (1984). *Experiential learning: Experience as the source of learning and development*. Prentice Hall.

Kosanovich, M., & Foorman, B. (2016). Professional learning communities facilitator's guide for the What Works Clearinghouse practice guide: Foundational skills to support reading for understanding in kindergarten through 3rd grade (REL 2016-227). U.S. Department of Education, Institute of Education Sciences, National Center for Education Evaluation and Regional Assistance, Regional Educational Laboratory Southeast. http://ies.ed.gov/ncee/edlabs

Lai, C., Zhang, W., & Chang, Y. (2020). Differentiated instruction enhances sixth-grade students' mathematics self-efficacy, learning motives, and problem-solving skills. *Social Behavior and Personality: An International Journal, 48*, 1–13. https://doi.org/10.2224/sbp.9094

Langelaan, B. N., Gaikhorst, L., Smets, W., & Oostdam, R. J. (2024). Differentiating instruction: Understanding the key elements for successful teacher preparation and development. *Teaching and Teacher Education, 140*. https://doi.org/10.1016/j.tate.2023.104464

Lay, M. M. M. (2024). Professional learning communities supporting professional development of teacher educators in Myanmar education colleges. *Pedagógusképzés, 22*(50), 35–54.

Liu, K. (2015). Critical reflection as a framework for transformational learning in teacher education. *Educational Research, 67*, 135–157. http://dx.doi.org/10.1080/00131911.2013.839546

Lockley, J., Jackson, N., Downing, A., & Roberts, J. (2017). University instructors' responses on implementation of differentiated instruction in teacher education programs. https://files.eric.ed.gov/fulltext/ED572728.pdf

Lortie, D. C. (1975). *Schoolteacher: A sociological study*. University of Chicago Press.

Loughram, J., & Berry, A. (2005). Modelling by teacher educators. *Teaching and Teacher Education*, *21*, 193–203. doi:10.1016/j.tate.2004.12.005

Lunenberg, M., Korthagen, F., & Swennen, A. (2007). The teacher educator as a role model. *Teaching and Teacher Education*, *23*, 586–601. doi:10.1016/j.tate.2006.11.001

Mackos, A. R., Casler, K., Tornwall, J., & O'Brien, T. (2023). Revitalizing the muddiest point for formative assessment and student engagement in a large class. *Nurse Educator*, *48*, 88–91. doi:10.1097/NNE.0000000000001295

Marks, A., Woolcott, G., & Markopoulos, C. (2021). Differentiating instruction: Development of a practice framework for and with secondary mathematics teachers. *International Electronic Journal of Mathematics Education*, *16*, em0657. https://doi.org/10.29333/iejme/11198

Massachusetts Department of Elementary and Secondary Education. (2023). *Student teachers*. Massachusetts Department of Elementary and Secondary Education. https://www.doe.mass.edu/edeffectiveness/talent-guide/student-teachers.html

Miftāḥ, M., Widiati, U., Wulyani, A., & Sharif, T. (2023). Strategies to develop preservice English teachers' pedagogical competence: A focus on critical reflection as a potential strategy. In *Proceedings of the 20th AsiaTEFL-68th TEFLIN-5th iNELTAL Conference (ASIATEFL 2022)*, 377–384. https://doi.org/10.2991/978-2-38476-054-1_33

Miller, L. R., Nelson, F. P., & Phillips, E. L. (2021). Exploring critical reflection in a virtual learning community in teacher education. *Reflective Practice*, *22*, 363–380. https://doi.org/10.1080/14623943.2021.1893165

Millington, M. (2025). Using instructional rounds as an alternative to traditional professional development. https://www.techlearning.com/news/using-instructional-rounds-as-an-alternative-to-traditional-professional-development

Missouri State University. (2024). *Teacher of record*. Missouri State University. https://www.missouristate.edu/ProfessionalEd/StudentTeaching/teacher-of-record.htm

Moll, L. C., Amanti, C., Neff, D., & Gonzalez, N. (1992). Funds of knowledge for teaching: Using a qualitative approach to connect homes and classrooms. *Theory into Practice*, *31*(2), 132–141.

Moore, E. J., & Bell, S. M. (2019). Is instructor (faculty) modeling an effective practice for teacher education? Insights and supports for new research. *Action in Teacher Education*, *41*, 325–343. https://doi.org/10.1080/01626620.2019.1622474

Moore, S. R. E. (2018). The impact of setting goals in elementary classrooms. *International Journal for Cross-Disciplinary Subjects in Education*, *9*, 3900–3905. https://doi.org/10.1007/s10639-021-10696-9

Morisano, D., Hirsh, J. B., Peterson, J. B., Pihl, R. O., & Shore, B. M. (2010). Setting, elaborating, and reflecting on personal goals improves academic performance. *Journal of Applied Psychology, 95*, 255–264. doi:https://doi.org/10.1037/a0018478

Morton, T., & Dyer, J. (2022). Differentiation matters! Six successful cross curricular strategies that provide process support for African American K–6th grade learners. *Texas Journal of Literacy Education, 9*, 34–43.

Mukagihana, J., Nsanganwimana, F., & Aurah, C. M. (2022). Effect of instructional methods on pre-service science teachers learning outcomes: A meta-analysis. *Education and Information Technologies, 27*, 2137–2163.

Murdoch, Y. D., Hyejung, L., & Kang, A. (2018). Learning students' given names benefits EMI classes. *English in Education, 52*, 225–247. https://doi.org/10.1080/04250494.2018.1509673

Nancekivell, S. E., Shah, P., & Gelman, S. A. (2020). Maybe they're born with it, or maybe it's experience: Toward a deeper understanding of the learning style myth. *Journal of Educational Psychology, 112*, 221–235. http://dx.doi.org/10.1037/edu0000366

National Science Teaching Association (NSTA). (2020). *2020 NSTA standards for science teacher preparation*. NSTA. https://www.nsta.org/nsta-standards-science-teacher-preparation

Nelson, F. L., Miller, L. R., & Yun, C. (2016). "It's OK to feel totally confused": Reflection without practice by preservice teachers in an introductory education course. *Reflective Practice, 17*, 648–661. http://dx.doi.org/10.1080/14623943.2016.1197113

Noddings, N. (2019). Concepts of care in teacher education. *Oxford Research Encyclopedia of Education*. https://doi.org/10.1093/acrefore/9780190264093.013.371

Ogle, D. (1986). KWL: A teaching model that develops active reading of expository text. *The Reading Teacher, 40*, 564–570.

Oo, C. Z., Alonzo, D., & Davison, C. (2023). Using a needs-based professional development program to enhance pre-service teacher assessment for learning literacy. *International Journal of Instruction, 16*(1), 781–800. https://doi.org/10.29333/iji.2023.16144a

Parsons, S. A., Dodman, S. L., & Burrowbridge, S. C. (2013). Broadening the view of differentiated instruction. *Phi Delta Kappan, 95*, 38–42.

Pashler, H., McDaniel, M., Rohrer, D., & Bjork, R. (2008). Learning styles: Concepts and evidence. *Psychological Science in the Public Interest, 9*(3), 105–119. https://doi.org/10.1111/j.1539-6053.2009.01038.x

Patall, E. A., & Zambrano, J. (2019). Facilitating student outcomes by supporting autonomy: Implications for practice and policy. *Policy Insights from the Behavioral and Brain Sciences, 6*(2), 115–122. https://doi.org/10.1177/2372732219862572

Porta, T., & Todd, N. (2022). Differentiated instruction within senior secondary curriculum frameworks: A small-scale study of teacher views from an independent South Australian school. *The Curriculum Journal, 33*, 570–586. https://doi.org/10.1002/curj.157

Preston, M., Subban, P., Suprayogi, M. N., Liyani, A. N., & Ratri, A. P. P. (2025). Differentiated instruction in higher education: The experience and perceptions of five academics. *Journal of Education and Learning (EduLearn), 19*, 1295–1306. https://doi.org/10.11591/edulearn.v19i3.21760

Puzio, K., Colby, G. T., & Algeo-Nichols, D. (2020). Differentiated literacy instruction: Boondoggle or best practice? *Review of Educational Research, 90*, 459–498. https://doi.org/10.3102/0034654320933536

Reeve, J., Ryan, R. M., Cheon, S. H., Matos, L., & Kaplan, H. (2022). *Supporting students' motivation: Strategies for success.* Routledge.

Reiner, C., & Willingham, D. (2010). The myth of learning styles. *Change: The Magazine of Higher Learning, 45*(5), 32–35. doi:10.1080/00091383.2010.503139

Roberts, J. L., & Inman, T. F. (2015). *Strategies for differentiating instruction: Best practices for the classroom* (3rd ed.). Prufrock Press.

Roiha, A. (2023). Broadening pre-service English language teachers' perceptions of differentiation relying on the 5D model. *The Teacher Educator, 58*(3), 289–306. https://doi.org/10.1080/08878730.2022.2126054

Ruys, I., Defruyt, S., Rots, I., & Aelterman, A. (2013). Differentiated instruction in teacher education: A case study of congruent teaching. *Teachers & Teaching: Theory & Practice, 19*, 93–107. http://dx.doi.org/10.1080/13540602.2013.744201

Sakellariou, M., & Polyxeni, M. (2019). Prospective kindergarten and primary school teachers' attitudes and beliefs on differentiated teaching during their teaching practice. *Journal of Advanced Research in Social Sciences.* https://doi.org/10.33422/jarss.2019.05.05

Samples, E. (2012, May 20). Why FCAT scores dropped like the backside of a camel's hump. *TC Palm.* https://archive.tcpalm.com/news/columnists/eve-samples-why-fcat-scores-dropped-like-the-backside-of-a-camels-hump-ep-382536976-343220572.html

Sandstrom, G. M. (2023). Even minimal student-instructor interactions may increase enjoyment in the classroom: Preliminary evidence that greeting your students may have benefits even if you can't remember their names. *PLoS One, 18*, e0288166. https://doi.org/10.1371/journal.pone.0288166

Santangelo, T., & Tomlinson, C. A. (2009) The application of differentiated instruction in postsecondary environments: Benefits, challenges, and future directions. *International Journal of Teaching and Learning in Higher Education, 20*, 307–323.

Scarparolo, G., & Subban, P. (2021). A systematic review of pre-service teachers' self-efficacy beliefs for differentiated instruction. *Teachers and Teaching, 27*, 753–766. https://doi.org/10.1080/13540602.2021.2007371

Shareefa, M. (2023). Demystifying the impact of teachers' qualification and experience on implementation of differentiated instruction. *International Journal of Instruction, 16*, 393–416. https://doi.org/10.29333/iji.2023.16122a

Shareefa, M., Moosa, V., Zin, R. M., Midawati, A., & Jawawi, R. (2019). Teachers' perceptions on differentiated instruction: Do experience, qualifications and challenges matter? *International Journal of Learning, Teaching, and Educational Research, 18*, 214–226. https://doi.org/10.26803/ijlter.18.8.13

Siech, C., García, C., Leyh, H., Schmid, H., Engl, T., Karakiewicz, P. I., Becker, A., Chun, F. K. H., Banek, S., & Kluth, L. (2022). Standardized evaluation of satisfaction within urology residents during clinical training: Implementation of a new urological residency rotation program at the university hospital Frankfurt. *Frontiers in Surgery, 9*. https://doi.org/10.3389/fsurg.2022.1038336

Silva-Padron, G., & McCann, M. (2023). 50-state comparison: Instructional time policies. *Education Commission of the States*. https://www.ecs.org/50-state-comparison-instructional-time-policies-2023

Sousa, D. A., & Tomlinson, C. A. (2018). *Differentiation and the brain: How neuroscience supports the learner-friendly classroom* (2nd ed.). ASCD.

South Dakota Legislature. (2023). Rule 67:42:01:05. General authority of the department to license and regulate. South Dakota Legislature. https://sdlegislature.gov/api/Rules/40447.html

Stanford, L. (2023). Every state now lets schools measure students' success based on mastery, not seat time. *Education Week*. https://www.edweek.org/policy-politics/every-state-now-lets-schools-measure-students-success-based-on-mastery-not-seat-time/2023/05

Stanley, T. (2022). *A teacher's toolbox for gifted education: 20 strategies you can use today to challenge gifted students*. Taylor & Francis.

Starck, J. R., O'Neil, K. M., & Richards, K. A. (2023). Preservice teachers' perceptions of and intentions to utilize assessment. *Curriculum Studies in Health and Physical Education, 15*, 324–339. https://doi.org/10.1080/25742981.2023.2240300

Subban, P., Suprayogi, M. N., Preston, M., Liyani, A. N., & Ratri, A. P. P. (2024). "Differentiation is sometimes a hit and miss": Educator perceptions of differentiation in the higher education sector. *The Asia-Pacific Education Researcher, 34*, 873–884. https://doi.org/10.1007/s40299-024-00904-8

Suprayogi, M. N., Vaicke, M., & Godwin, R. (2017). Teachers and their implementation of differentiated instruction in the classroom. *Teaching and Teacher Education, 67*, 291–301. https://doi.org/10.1016/j.tate.2017.06.020

Sweller, J. (1988). Cognitive load during problem solving: Effects on learning. *Cognitive Science, 12*, 257–285. https://doi.org/10.1207/s15516709cog1202_4

Szocik, K., Gerry, M. A., & Nagro, S. A. (2021). The impact of reflective practice on teacher candidates' attitudes towards individuals with disabilities and professional identity. *Reflective Practice, 22*, 739–752. https://doi.org/10.1080/14623943.2021.1967735

Tomlinson, C. A. (2014) *The differentiated classroom: Responding to the needs of all learners* (2nd ed.). ASCD.

Tomlinson, C. A. (2017). *How to differentiate instruction in academically diverse classrooms* (3rd ed.). ASCD.

Travers, C. J., Morisano, S., & Locke, E. A. (2014). Self-reflection, growth goals, and academic outcomes: A qualitative study. *British Journal of Educational Psychology, 85*, 224–241. https://doi.org/10.1111/bjep.12059

Valiandes, S., & Neophytou, L. (2018). Teachers' professional development for differentiated instruction in mixed-ability classrooms: Investigating the impact of a development program on teachers' professional learning and in students' achievement. *Teacher Development, 22*, 123–138. https://doi.org/10.1080/13664530.2017.1338196

van Geel, M., Keuning, T., & Safar, I. (2022). How teachers develop skills for implementing differentiated instruction: Helpful and hindering factors. *Teaching and Teacher Education: Leadership and Professional Development, 1*. https://doi.org/10.1016/j.tatelp.2022.100007

van Geel, M., Keuning, T., Frerejean, J., Dolmans, D., van Merrienboer, J., & Visscher, A. J. (2019). Capturing the complexity of differentiated instruction. *School Effectiveness and School Improvement, 30*, 51–67. https://doi.org/10.1080/09243453.2018.1539013

van Geel, M., Keuning, T., Meutstege, K., de Vries, J., Visscher, A., Wolterinck, C., Schildkamp, K., & Poortman, C. (2023). Adapting teaching to students' needs: What does it require from teachers? In R. Maulana, M. Helms-Lorenz, & R. M. Klassen (Eds.), *Effective teaching around the world*, 723–736. Springer. https://doi.org/10.1007/978-3-031-31678-4_33

Wan, S. W. (2017). Differentiated instruction: Are Hong Kong in-service teachers ready? *Teachers and Teaching: Theory and Practice, 23*, 284–311. http://dx.doi.org/10.1080/13540602.2016.1204289

Wang, Y., Ko, J., & Hu, Q. (2022). How would preservice teachers with deeper reflection emerge as teacher leaders? *ECNU Review of Education, 6*, 237–260. https://doi.org/10.1177/20965311221142892

Wang, Y., Zhang, Y., Kiu, L., Cui, J., Wang, J., Shum, D. H. K., van Amelsvoort, T., & Chan, R. C. K. (2017). A meta-analysis of working memory impairments in autism spectrum disorders. *Neuropsychology Review, 27*, 46–61. https://doi.org/10.1007/s11065-016-9336-y

Ward, J. R., & McCotter, S. S. (2004). Reflection as a visible outcome for preservice teachers. *Teaching and Teacher Education, 20*, 243–257. https://doi.org/10.1016/j.tate.2004.02.004

Watts-Taffe, S., Laster, B. P., Broach, L., Marinak, B., Connor, C. M., & Walker-Dalhouse, D. (2012). Differentiated instruction: Making informed teacher decisions. *The Reading Teacher, 66*, 303–314. https://doi.org/10.1002/TRTR.01126

Westman, L. (2018). *Student-driven differentiation: 8 steps to harmonize learning in the classroom*. Corwin.

Wherfel, Q. M., Monda-Amaya, L., & Shriner, J. G. (2022). General education teacher practices: Assessment, decision-making and the influence of co-teaching. *Preventing School Failure: Alternative Education for Children and Youth, 66*, 42–51. https://doi.org/10.1080/1045988X.2021.1934650

Whinnery, S. B., Fogle, K. C., Stark, J. C., & Whinnery, K. W. (2020). Building collaborative teacher education: Integrating UDL through a faculty learning community. *Journal of Practitioner Research, 5*, Article 5. https://doi.org/10.5038/2379-9951.5.2.1161

Whitehead, P. M. (2023). *Autonomy-supportive teaching in higher education*. Rowman & Littlefield.

Winebrenner, S. (1992). *Teaching gifted kids in the regular classroom*. Free Spirit.

Wininger, S. R., & Norman, A. D. (2005). Teacher candidate's exposure to formative assessment in educational psychology textbooks: A content analysis. *Educational Assessment, 10*, 19–37.

Woelmer, W., Bradley, L., Haber, L., Klinges, D., Lewis, A., Mohr, E., Torrens, C. L., Wheeler, K. I., & Willson, A. (2021). Ten simple rules for training yourself in an emerging field. *PloS Computational Biology, 17*(10), e1009440. https://doi.org/10.1371/journal.pcbi.1009440

Woods, D., Poe, L., Brooks, N., Korzaan, M., & Hulshult, A. (2024). Assessing student focus areas for self-directed metacognition and self-improvement. *Journal of Effective Teaching in Higher Education, 7*, 96–117.

Yan, Z., Li, Z., Yang, M., Yang, L., & Lao, H. (2021). A systematic review on factors influencing teachers' intentions regarding formative assessment. *Assessment in Education: Principles, Policy & Practice, 28*, 228–260. https://doi.org/10.1080/0969594X.2021.1884042

Yee, B. C., Abdullah, T., & Nawi, A. M. (2022). Exploring pre-service teachers' reflective practice through an analysis of six-stage framework in reflective journals. *Reflective Practice, 23*, 552–564. https://doi.org/10.1080/14623943.2022.2071246

Yenmez, A. A., & Özpınar, I. (2017). Pre-service education on differentiated instruction: Elementary teacher candidates' competences and opinions on the process. *Journal of Education and Practice, 8*, 87–93.

Yeo, S. C., Lai, C. K. Y., Tan, J., Lim, S., Chandramoghan, Y., Tan, T. K., & Gooley, J. J. (2023). Early morning university classes are associated with impaired sleep and academic performance. *Nature Human Behavior, 7*, 502–514. https://doi.org/10.1038/s41562-023-01531-x

Zeichner, K., & Liu, K. Y. (2010). A critical analysis of reflection as a goal for teacher education. In N. Lyons (Ed.), *Handbook of reflection and reflective inquiry: Mapping a way of knowing for professional reflective inquiry*, 67–84. Springer.

Zeichner, K., Payne, K., & Brayko, K. (2014). Democratizing teacher education. *Journal of Teacher Education, 66*(2), 122–135. https://doi.org/10.1177/0022487114560908

Zelalem, A., Melesse, S., & Seifu, A. (2022). Teacher educators' self-efficacy and perceived practices of differentiated instruction in Ethiopian primary teacher education programs: Teacher education colleges in amhara regional state in focus. *Cogent Education, 9*. https://doi.org/10.1080/2331186X.2021.2018909

Zhang, Y. S. D., & Noels, K. A. (2021). The frequency and importance of accurate heritage name pronunciation for post-secondary international students in Canada. *Journal of International Students, 11*, 608–627. doi:10.32674/jis.v11i3.2232

Zhu, G., & Chen, M. (2022). Positioning preservice teachers' reflections and I-positions in the context of teaching practicum: A dialogical-self theory approach. *Teaching and Teacher Education, 117*. https://doi.org/10.1016/j.tate.2022.103734

Index

3-2-1 charts 42–3
100-point project 133, 134–41

accountability 63–4
actionable feedback 79
additional check-ins 126–7
adjusting content 87–8
affordances 90–1
anchor spaces 66
anonymous feedback 70, 81
anticipation guides 33–5, 48–9
assessment 29–57
    3-2-1 charts 42–3
    anticipation guides 33–5, 48–9
    co-construction 64
    design 160
    entrance cards 36, 49–50
    exit tickets 42, 48, 49–50
    five-most-difficult questions 41
    formative 29–30
    four-corners activity 37–8
    goal setting 50–3
    instruction-embedded 41–5
    journal prompts 36
    K-W-L charts 43–4
    methodologies 29–30
    mind maps 39–41
    muddiest point activity 44–5
    for planning 46–50
    pre-assessments 31–41
    purpose of 29, 31
    as separate from teaching 30–1
    summative 29
    triage self-assessment 45
    vocabulary charts 32–3, 46–8
    vote-with-your-feet activity 38–9

assignments
    co-construction 64
    design 160
    due dates 60–1
    revisions and resubmission 61–2
audiobooks 90–1
autonomy 63–5

background knowledge 13
belonging 72–3
breakout rooms 68
bridges, Dual Role Reflection Model 23–6

case studies 63, 110–12
challenges 8–10, 15–16
check-ins, additional 126–7
checklists, major assignments 105–7
choice boards 132–52
    100-point project 133, 134–41
    rubrics 133, 139–41, 146, 150–1
    tic-tac-toe 133, 142–7
chunking tasks 104–5
classroom environment 59–65
    anchor spaces 66
    autonomy 63–5
    collaborative spaces 66–7
    expectations 60–5, 69–70
    grouping strategies 75–8
    physical characteristics 65–6
    quiet spaces 66–7
    risk-taking 62–3
    setting the stage 71–5
    student feedback 78–81
    think time 71
    virtual 67–70
    welcoming students 67

clinical placements 160–1, 164, 173–4
clock buddies 76
co-construction 64
collaboration across faculties 157
collaborative activities 62–4, 75–9
collaborative model analysis 109
collaborative spaces 66–7
communications 163–4
compacting 88
comparative models 109–10
complexity, process differentiation 110–14
concept maps 39–41
  see also mind maps
connecting statements, Dual Role Reflection Model 23–6
constructive feedback 62, 78–9
content differentiation 85–101
  adjusting tasks 87–8
  formats 87
  guided notes 88–9
  learning contracts 95–8
  materials 86–8
  methods 88–91
  modalities 87
  scaffolding 90
  small-group instruction 90
  student research 90
  task charts 91–5
  technology affordances 90–1
  texts 86–7
Conversation Calendar 79–80
co-teaching 161
course mapping 159–60
CRT see culturally responsive teaching
culturally responsive teaching (CRT) 4–5, 65, 85, 128–9

DI see differentiated instruction
differentiated instruction (DI)
  benefits of 5–7
  key concepts 2–5
  modeling 7–8
differentiation
  by content see content differentiation
  by environment see environment
  by process see process differentiation
  by product see product differentiation
directions, staging 104–5

discussion boards 69
diversity, of strengths 13–16
Dual Role Reflection Model 20–6
  bridges 23–6
  graphic organizer 168–9
  lenses 22–3
due dates 60–1, 115–16

effort, to complete a task 12
engagement 63–4
enrichment 12, 15
entrance cards 36, 49–50
environment 59–84
  autonomy 63–5
  classroom 59–65
  collaborative spaces 66–7
  expectations 60–5, 69–70
  grouping strategies 75–8
  physical 65–6
  quiet spaces 66–7
  risk-taking 62–3
  setting the stage 71–5
  strategies 65–71
  student feedback 78–81
  think time 71
  virtual 67–70
  welcoming students 67
equality, vs. equity 12
equity, vs. equality 12
exit tickets 42, 48, 49–50
expectations 60–5, 69–70
expert groups 116–17
expertise 156–8
explicit modeling 7–8, 17–18
extension opportunities 103–4

faculty collaboration 157, 159, 161–2
faculty development 155–67
  assignments and assessments 160
  clinical placements 160–1, 164, 173–4
  collaboration 157, 159, 161–2
  course mapping 159–60
  expertise 156–8
  modeling 162
  partnerships 164
  program design 159–64
  resources 158, 163–4
faculty expertise 156–7

Index 189

feedback
    actionable 79
    anonymous 70, 81
    constructive 62, 78–9
    Conversation Calendar 79–80
    inviting 78–81
    peers 63–4, 68
    stop, start, continue 80–1
five-most-difficult questions pre-assessment 41
flexible grouping 75–9
flexible pacing 115–16
formative assessment 29–30
formats, of content 87
four-corners activity 37–8
front-loading 107–8

goal setting 50–3
    differentiation by product 127–8
    revisiting 53, 127–8
    SMART 51–3
graphic organizers 117–19
grouping
    clock buddies 76
    preassigned 76–7
    random 77–8
    strategies 75–8
guest experts 157–8
guided notes 88–9

hybrid courses 67–70

icebreakers 72–3
IEPs *see* individualized education programs
"in the desks" lens 22–4
individualized education programs (IEPs) 14–15
initial questionnaires 74–5
"in my experience" lens 22–4
"in the profession" lens 23–6
inquiry charts 118–19
instruction-embedded assessments 41–5
    3-2-1 charts 42–3
    exit tickets 42, 48, 49–50
    K-W-L charts 43–4
    muddiest point activity 44–5
    triage self-assessment 45
interdisciplinary collaboration 157, 159, 161–2

interpersonal products 125
intrinsic motivation 17
introductory peer interviews 72

jigsaw activity 116–17
journal prompts 36

K-W-L charts 43–4

late-work policies 60–1
learning contracts 95–8
lenses, Dual Role Reflection Model 20, 22–3
letters, to student caregivers 18
low-stakes activities 62–3

Major Assignment Step Checklists 105–7
materials, content differentiation 86–8
matrix charts 117–18
memories, on mugs 73–4
mentorship 157
menu assignments 132–52
    see also choice boards
microteaching 162
mind maps 39–41
misconceptions 15–16
modalities
    of content 87
    differentiation by product 124–5
modeling 7–8, 17–18
    faculty development 162
    processes 108–10
    risk-taking 62
motivation, intrinsic 17
muddiest point activity 44–5
mugs, memories on 73–4
multimedia resources, front-loading 107–8
multimodal products 124–5

names, pronunciation 71–2
name tents 73
neurodivergent individuals 104–5
norms 69–70

one-on-one meetings 126
online courses 67–70
ownership 63

pacing 115–16
partial directions 104–5
partial models 109
partnerships 164
peer feedback 63–4, 68
peer interviews 72
peer-to-peer interaction
    grouping strategies 75–8
    online 68–9
performative products 125
personal strengths 13–16
physical environment 65–6
planning, by assessment 46–50
PLCs *see* professional learning
    communities
practice questions 114–15
pre-assessments 31–41
    anticipation guides 33–5, 48–9
    entrance cards 36, 49–50
    five-most-difficult questions 41
    four-corners activity 37–8
    journal prompts 36
    mind maps 39–41
    vocabulary charts 32–3, 46–8
    vote-with-your-feet activity 38–9
preassigned groups 76–7
preservice teachers (PSTs)
    Dual Role Reflection Model 20–6
    initial introduction 11
    inviting feedback 78–81
    misconceptions 15–16
    peer interviews 72
    questionnaires 74–5
    reflection 18–26
    sense of belonging 72–3
    supporting understanding 16–18
    welcoming 67
prior knowledge 13
process differentiation 103–22
    case studies 110–12
    complexity 110–14
    front-loading 107–8
    general strategies 104–16
    graphic organizers 117–19
    jigsaw activity 116–17
    major assignment checklists 105–7
    modeling 108–10
    pacing 115–16
    practice questions 114–15

    specific strategies 116–20
    staging directions 104–5
    technology tools 119–20
    tiered activities 113–14
product differentiation 123–54
    culturally responsive 128–9
    general strategies 126–9
    goal setting 127–8
    modalities 124–5
    RAFT writing prompts 129–32
professional disposition 20
professionalization 19
professional learning communities (PLCs)
    156
proficiencies
    background knowledge 13
    personal strengths 13–16
    time to reach 12
program design 159–64
    course mapping 159–60
program-level learning communities 156
pronunciation of names 71–2
PSTs *see* preservice teachers
pulse checks 70
purpose, of assessment 29, 31

questionnaires, initial 74–5
quiet spaces 66–7

RAFT writing prompts 129–32
random grouping 77–8
rationales 64
reflection 18–26
    dual role model 20–6
    product choice 127
    professional disposition 20
    and professionalization 19
    questions 170–4
    revisiting goals 53
    self-focus 19–20
relevance 16–17
resource provision 158, 163–4
restaurant menu choice board 147–52
resubmissions 61–2
revisions 61–2
revisiting, goals 53, 127–8
risk-taking 62–3
rubrics, choice boards 132–3, 139–41, 146,
    150–1

scaffolding 90, 119–20, 123, 126
scaffolding statements, Dual Role Reflection Model 23–6
self-assessment
    product choice 127
    triage 45
    see also reflection
self-efficacy 61–5
sense of belonging 72–3
setting the stage 71–5
    memories on mugs 73–4
    name tents 73
    peer interviews 72
    pronunciation of names 71–2
    stand up/hand up 72–3
    student questionnaires 74–5
simulations 162
small-group instruction 90
small-group meetings 127
SMART goals 51–3
soft deadlines 115–16
speech-to-text technologies 119–20
staged directions 104–5
stand up/hand up activity 72–3
station-based learning 103
stop, start, continue feedback 80–1
strategies
    content differentiation 86–98
    differentiation by process 104–20
    differentiation by product 126–52
    environmental 65–71
    grouping 75–8
    physical environment 65–6
    student feedbacl 78–81

strengths, diversity of 13–16
student choice 103
student questionnaires 74–5
student research 90
success for all 61
summaries 88–9
summative assessment 29

targeted learning 87–8
task charts 91–5
teaching, and assessment 30–1
team work 62–3, 75–9
technology affordances 90–1, 119–20
texts 86–7
text-to-speech technologies 119–20
think time 71
tic-tac-toe choice board 133, 142–4
tiered activities 113–14
time, to complete a task 12
triage self-assessment 45

videos
    front-loading 107–8
    walkthroughs 109
virtual environments 67–70
virtual office hours 70–1
vocabulary charts 32–3, 46–8
vote-with-your-feet activity 38–9

walkthrough videos 109
welcoming students 67
working memory 104–5
workshops 162
written products 124

Author Biography

Sarah E. Pennington is an associate professor in education at Montana State University in Bozeman, Montana. Her teaching experience spans K–12 public schools, private colleges, and large public universities. Her research interests include middle-grade education, teacher education, and adolescent literacy motivation.